CUT COSTS
NOT CORNERS

CUT COSTS
NOT CORNERS

A practical guide to staying competitive
and improving profits

Colin Barrow

KoganPage

LONDON PHILADELPHIA NEW DELHI

Publisher's note

Every possible effort has been made to ensure that the information contained in this book is accurate at the time of going to press, and the publishers and author cannot accept responsibility for any errors or omissions, however caused. No responsibility for loss or damage occasioned to any person acting, or refraining from action, as a result of the material in this publication can be accepted by the editor, the publisher or the author.

First published in Great Britain and the United States in 2010 by Kogan Page Limited

120 Pentonville Road	525 South 4th Street, #241	4737/23 Ansari Road
London N1 9JN	Philadelphia PA 19147	Daryaganj
United Kingdom	USA	New Delhi 110002
www.koganpage.com		India

© Colin Barrow, 2010

ISBN 978 0 7494 5976 5
E-ISBN 978 0 7494 5977 2

British Library Cataloguing-in-Publication Data

A CIP record for this book is available from the British Library.

Library of Congress Cataloging-in-Publication Data

Barrow, Colin.
    Cut costs not corners : a practical guide to staying competitive and improving profits / Colin Barrow.
        p. cm.
    ISBN 978-0-7494-5976-5 – ISBN 978-0-7494-5977-2 (ebk)   1. Cost control.
2. Corporate profits.   3. Corporations – Finance – Management.   I. Title.
    HD47.3.B36   2010
    658.15′52–dc22

                                                                        2009048334

Typeset by Graphicraft Limited, Hong Kong
Printed and bound in India by Replika Press Pvt Ltd

Contents

Figures

Tables

Introduction

The saying, 'Tell me what you eat and I will tell you what you are' ('Dis-moi ce que tu manges, je te dirai ce que tu es'), coined by Anthelme Brillat-Savarin (1826), a French lawyer and politician, provided an expression that has been enthusiastically adopted by chefs and nutritionists ever since. Chris Young, founder of The Rainmaker Group (www.therainmakergroupinc.com) in Bismarck, North Dacata, an employee relations company, has a very similar motto. He reckons that you live your job title and, whatever your title is, that's what you'll be. If a receptionist is called director of first impressions, Young believes they will understand that the way they greet people and answer the phone really matters. Setting an appropriate example, Young's business card is headed Founder and Difference Maker, a title he even uses for signing off the accounts.

The business world is awash with impressive titles. CEO (chief executive officer), CFO (chief financial officer) and CTO (chief technology officer), for example, all give a reasonable impression of what is expected. Recently some more adventurous companies have extended the range of job titles. At America Online, the head of the business's matchmaking service is called CEO of Love, whilst Google has appointed a CCO (chief culture officer) whose mission is to retain the company's unique culture and keep the Googlers happy. The person in charge of organizing Berkshire Hathaway's world-famous annual shareholder meeting is the director of chaos, and further down the chain of command Reed Employment is on the lookout for a graduate football bet placer. The only downside to that job being that due to the timing of football matches, working weekends is standard.

Southwest Airlines have a DCA (director of culture activities), whose role includes generally keeping morale up, throwing

barbeques and raising money for employees going through hard-
ships. That role probably won't appear high on Ryanair's list
of must-have board members any time soon. One that might,
however, is a CCCO. Don't be too concerned if you haven't come
across that acronym; as far as I'm aware, no one holds that title.
Whilst Google has 78,200,000 entries for chief executive, there are
no listings at all for chief cost-cutting officer, which is a pity as it
is arguably one of the most important jobs going. It's not that
organizations don't see cost cutting as important; it's just that
they don't see it as a job.

Google discovers cost cutting

In July 2009, whilst most technology companies were reporting a significant collapse in profits and the motor and banking industries were simply
collapsing, Google managed to report that earnings for the second quarter of the year were up 19 per cent compared with the previous year.
Their success was not attributed either to increased revenues or new
products; True Gmail, Google Docs, Google Calendar and other web
applications had all played a part in lifting sales revenue by around
3 per cent, but that left the lion's share of profit growth to a new and
hitherto unused (by Google at least) business strategy.

The secret formula lay in cutting costs. Out went bottled water and a
host of other perks. Programmes were instituted throughout the company
to ensure cost effectiveness. For example, their food service team closely
examined café usage, food consumption and labour costs to find areas
where efficiency could be improved without compromising food quality
and nutrition. Cafeteria opening hours were trimmed back and the practice of those working late taking the dinner provided in the office to eat
at home later was discouraged. Afternoon tea on Tuesdays for all and
sundry was suspended, though to keep morale up the company stated
that there may be occasional surprise 'snack attacks' in the future.
Capital expenditure was slashed by 80 per cent and due to natural
wastage the company ended the quarter with fewer employees.

Who this book is for

This book is NOT another of the many worthy manuals on costing full of intricate arguments on how to allocate overheads and explanations on the role of cost centres, codes and recovery methods. Sure, you will need a basic grasp of finance, but no more than anyone in business should have or be able to acquire with only a modest effort and willingness to do so.

The clue to the guiding principle of the book lies in the title: cutting costs, not corners. Cutting costs is not about exposing customers, employees, shareholders, suppliers, the local community or indeed anyone to undue risks. So don't expect to find tips on how to fly-tip hazardous waste, extend the shelf life of fire extinguishers or push the fine print of contractual relationships to the stratosphere. There won't be anything much on introducing value coffee to the canteen, eliminating lunch breaks or removing hazard guards from machinery to speed up work flow – all cost-cutting ideas routinely applied in some businesses – along with skimping on health and safety checks or letting anyone drive the forklift truck.

The book is for executives, managers, directors, shareholders and business owners of every size and type of enterprise and those in both the private and public sectors who want to apply or continue to apply the three enduring management principles: be frugal, be honest and be prepared. In fact, anyone who spends someone else's money or has someone spend theirs should have a lifetime proactive concern with keeping costs on a permanent southward trend. In short, the book is a tool kit for the would-be CCCO. It contains:

- a framework for analysing and understanding costs and their behaviours;
- proven ideas that can save an organization cash from day one;
- practical techniques and processes for implementing cost-reduction programmes that are tried and tested;
- cost-cutting methods for times of crisis.

Myth 1: cost cutting is for times of crisis only

Cost cutting is seen as a one-off task usually in response to some external crisis. The credit crunch of 2008–10 is a good example of when almost every type of organization had costs squeezed hard. Google Insights noted that the use of the term 'cost cutting' in web searches quadrupled between December 2006 and February 2009.

Nothing is considered sacred in a downturn and almost anything can be sacrificed to ensure corporate survival. The people usually charged with doing the squeezing are the CEO, who sets the target, and the CFO, who decides whose pips will be squeezed the hardest. At best a task force is assembled to carry out the work, but more usually the role of Mr Nasty is left to the CFO.

Once the crisis is past, everyone breathes a sigh of relief and gets back to business as usual. For CEOs that usually means vastly overpaying for acquisitions. The acquisition of Dutch bank ABN AMRO by a consortium led by RBS (Royal Bank of Scotland), for €70 billion (£61.5 billion) in July 2007, some €9 billion more than rival Barclays felt the business was worth, is perhaps the most conspicuous example of overpaying to buy a rival. This, the biggest, and almost certainly the worst, banking takeover in history, was carried out in weeks by Sir Fred Goodwin, chief executive of the Royal Bank of Scotland, sweeping aside a bid assembled by Barclays chief executive, John Varley, who had carried out months of painstaking due diligence in arriving at a valuation.

Paradoxically, if CEOs and CFOs could just be a little more patient and carry out more of their acquisitions during recessions, they could cut this type of cost significantly whilst improving their chance of having a successful outcome, itself an unusual event in the M&A (mergers and acquisitions) field. A study of nearly 1,000 mainly industrial US companies over an 18-year period (1982–99) that included the US recession of 1990–1 concluded that the most successful companies held their fire during the expansion stage of the economic cycle, making 64 per cent fewer acquisitions than their peers. But during the recession, whilst competitors brought their deal-making activity nearly to a halt, the most successful firms stepped up their acquisitions, often making 'transactions that offered greater opportunity to shape industries'. Who knows, the Lloyd's TSB acquisition of HBOS announced in September 2008 could turn out to have been a prime example of an opportunistic mega acquisition with the potential to reshape an industry that could only happen in a major downturn. But at 232p a share, Lloyds TSB still paid four times more than they need have done, had they waited just a few more weeks.

Xstrata vs Anglo American: a battle between cost savers

On 23 June 2009, Anglo American, the South Africa-based mining group with its headquarters in London, rebuffed a 'friendly' approach from Swiss rival Xstrata. Both companies had similar market capitalizations and turnovers of $26.3 billion and $27.9 billion respectively. The deal on offer to shareholders was a merger of equals with no cash changing hands. The logic was to create annual cost savings of between $700 million and $1.7 billion (£428 million–£1 billion) if overlapping businesses were combined, logistics and distribution shared and a single lean head office created. The companies have several large shareholders in common who were enthusiastic about the deal.

Cynthia Carroll, Anglo's CEO, and her board took just two hours to reject the approach, stating that they were in the middle of a cost-cutting drive that was expected to produce savings of $2 billion (£1.21 billion) by 2011. Half of those cost savings were expected to come from operational efficiencies and half from a project to coordinate group procurement. Anglo also announced plans to reduce 2009 capital expenditure by $4.5 billion (£2.72 billion).

Analysts were divided on the merits of the merger. Some saw the proposed cost savings as virtually bankable. Others felt the corporate cultures would be difficult to merge and so cost savings might be difficult to realize. Xstrata, headed by Mick Davis, has a reputation for its lean decentralized structure employing just 40,000 people compared to Anglo's 105,000. Its meteoric growth since 2002 has been fuelled largely by an aggressive acquisition spree. Anglo, with dual management structures in Johannesburg and London, is a more complicated business and one that has cut 19,000 jobs globally over the past two years.

Myth 2: cost cutting is just another word for downsizing

By the 1980s, downsizing had become a ubiquitous feature of many organizations in the United States and elsewhere in the developed world. By the 1990s it had become the strategy of choice when dealing with a cyclical business downturn, merger or acquisition, or some other economic threat. In the area of downsizing it is usually the CEO and the human resources department that come into play. Cutting staff numbers may be the strategy of choice but it is not one that is certain to succeed. There are hidden costs in any downsizing activity, such as increased staff turnover, lower morale and reduced effort, which in turn reduce productivity and lower commitment. These hidden costs often limit the value of downsizing as a cost-reduction strategy. A 2006 study on airline resiliency – the capability to 'recover from or adjust easily to misfortune or change' – after the 9/11 terrorist attacks in 2001 proved this point eloquently. It identified a significant correlation between the use of downsizing as a cost-cutting strategy and the recovery in share price. Southwest Airlines laid off no employees, and their share price recovered by 90 per cent within four years. United Airlines cut 20 per cent of employees, and its share price recovered by only 11 per cent over the same period.

A wide-ranging survey of studies on the effectiveness of downsizing in all economic climates published in 2008 in the *Society for the Advancement of Management* journal offers these two robust conclusions:

- Most firms adopting downsizing strategies do not reap economic and organizational benefits.
- Non-downsized firms financially outperform downsized forms in the short, medium, and long run.

The authors of this study went on to recommend that any organization considering using downsizing as a means of cutting costs should:

- have plans in place before a downturn (or other event) happens;
- communicate honestly, openly and quickly;
- Use imaginative, varied and agreed strategies to take out cost over the period of the downturn rather than resorting to redundancies, whether compulsory or voluntary.

Fact: cost cutting is forever

This book has two basic messages. First, cost cutting is a permanent management process, and by concentrating its execution only during periods of distress or economic downturn an organization can miss out on some major opportunities to pay less for more. Cost cutting also plays a vital role in ensuring a business becomes or remains competitive, an argument expanded on in Chapter 1. Staying competitive means that there are fewer reasons for knee-jerk reactions when the going gets tough.

The second message is that savaging headcount alone as a means of cutting costs can be counterproductive. In any event, there are many more rewarding areas to explore to keep costs on an ever downward curve. In most of these areas it will be easier to enthuse, motivate and even reward employees to play a full role as participants rather than becoming hostile guerillas fighting a war of attrition to prevent change at any price.

Cisco Systems

Cisco, a Fortune 100 transnational company and the worldwide leader in providing hardware, software and service offerings that provide networking solutions for the internet, is always striving to build lower costs into its product offerings. Unsurprisingly the company is an enthusiastic consumer of its own products. They use wikis, social networking and other low-cost web-based collaboration services, all enabled by their routers. But it is TelePresence, developed over a seven-year period whilst economies were booming, that Cisco believes to be a long-term winner. TelePresence is a video-conferencing system that captures subtle nuances such as body language and tone of voice and gives users the real feeling of being in the same room together. Some 5,500 TelePresence meetings take place throughout Cisco worldwide every week, enabling them to cut their annual travel budget by $290 million (£175 million) – just over 50 per cent.

How to use this book

There are no rich seams to mine in the search for ways to cut costs that apply universally to all types of business. Some businesses employ relatively small amounts of capital, typically consultancies of all types, law firms and distributors. Even firms that have most of their costs in the people area can have quite different issues when it comes to controlling those costs. A call centre and a law firm both employ people but the productivity potential and strategies for harvesting extra productivity will be very different from one to the other. Some firms are heavy on capital and employ few but expensive people; oil exploration and medical research are examples here. Others still are heavy on both capital and people: for example, manufacturers in general.

So rather than trying to pre-empt where you might start looking for areas in which to cut costs, this book runs down the balance sheet and profit and loss account (income statement), using those as the skeletons around which to explore areas for intelligent, organized and systematic cost cutting. These reports are used because all businesses have them. As such they are a convenient way to apply a universal yardstick to all types of venture as well as being tools to examine past, current and future performance, and to compare and contrast the performance of different organizations from which valuable information may be gleaned.

Of course, you can just as easily use the index to dive straight into a particular area – say, negotiating with suppliers, reducing the tax take or cutting bad debts – if you have specific areas of priority.

1

Whose cost is it anyway?

- Where cost meets activity;
- Understanding the components of cost;
- Appreciating the cost-cutting framework;
- Why frugal is good;
- The strategic implications of cost.

At first glance the answer to the question in the title of this chapter is that all costs are created by the organization, so that's where the buck stops. Whilst in a narrow sense that logic can't be faulted, the answer sidesteps what actions and events really drive costs. Not many of us set out just to incur costs. We usually have those decisions forced on us by the task in hand. After all, unless we buy in raw material, pay staff and employ equipment, we would have nothing to sell. In fact, the more successful we are at selling, the higher the costs we will actually incur.

To answer the question properly we need to know a bit more about the nature of costs, how they are incurred, which costs are good and, all other things being equal, which costs we should have more of and which are rather less desirable and should be discouraged or even eliminated.

The nature of cost

At first glance the problem is simple. Costs appear essentially the same in nature, in that they all tend to reduce a business's capacity to make a profit. They are best dealt with by ensuring revenues more than cover them, that is, money coming in from business activity. So just add up all the costs and charge a bit more. The more you charge above your costs, provided the customers keep on buying, the more profit you make. Unfortunately, as soon as you start to do the sums, the problem gets a little more complex. For a start, not all costs have the same characteristics. Some costs, for example, do not change, however much you sell. If you are running a shop, or a chain of shops for that matter, the rent and rates are relatively constant figures, completely independent of the volume of your sales. On the other hand, the cost of the products sold from those shops is completely dependent on volume. The more you sell, the more it costs you to buy in stock.

Table 1.1 Example of cost in total

	£/$/€
Monthly rent and rates for shop	2,500
Cost of 1,000 units of volume of product	1,000
Total costs	3,500

You can't really add up the two types of costs until you have made an assumption about volume – how much you plan to sell. Look at the simple example in Table 1.1. Until we decide to buy, and we hope sell, 1,000 units of our product, we cannot total the costs. With the volume hypothesized we can arrive at a cost per unit of product as shown in Table 1.2.

Table 1.2 Example of cost per unit

Total costs £/$/€	divided by number of units	=	unit cost £/$/€
3,500	1,000	=	3.50

Now, provided we sell out all 1,000 units at or above 3.50 per unit, we will at least cover our costs. But that is a risky assumption. Suppose we do not sell all the 1,000 units; what then? With a selling price of 4.50 we could, in theory, make a profit of 1,000 if we sell all 1,000 units. That is, a total sales revenue of 4,500, minus total costs of 3,500. But if we only sell 500 units, our total revenue drops to 2,250 and we actually lose 1,250 (total revenue 2,250 – total costs 3,500). So at one level of sales a selling price of 4.50 is satisfactory to cover costs, and at another it is a disaster. This very simple example shows that all those decisions are intertwined. Costs, sales volume, selling prices and profits are all linked together. A decision taken in any one of these areas has an impact on the other areas. To understand the relationship between these factors, we need a picture or model of how they link up. Before we can build up this model, we need some more information on each of the component parts of cost.

The components of cost

Understanding the behaviour of costs as the trading patterns in a business change is an area of vital importance to decisions on which costs to cut and how to cut them. It is this 'dynamic' nature in every business that makes good cost decisions the key to survival. The example showed that if the situation was static and predictable, a profit was certain, but that if any one component in the equation was not a certainty (in the example it was volume), then the situation was quite different.

To see how costs behave under changing conditions we first have to identify the different types of cost.

Fixed costs

Fixed costs are costs that happen, by and large, whatever the level of activity. For example, the cost of buying a car is the same whether it is driven 100 miles a year or 20,000 miles. The same is also true of the road tax, the insurance and any extras, such as a sat nav or entertainment centre.

In a business, as well as the cost of buying cars there are other fixed costs such as plant, equipment, computers, desks and telephones. But certain less tangible items can also be fixed costs: for example, rent, rates, insurance, etc, which are usually set quite independent of how successful or otherwise a business is.

Costs such as most of those mentioned above are fixed irrespective of the timescale under consideration. Other costs, such as those of employing people, whilst theoretically variable in the short term, in practice are fixed. In other words, if sales demand goes down and a business needs fewer people, the costs cannot be shed for several weeks (notice, holiday pay, redundancy, etc). Also, if the people involved are highly skilled or expensive to recruit and train (or in some other way particularly valuable) and the downturn looks a short one, it may not be cost effective to reduce those short-run costs in line with falling demand. So viewed over a period of weeks and months, labour is a fixed cost whilst over a longer period it may not be fixed.

Variable costs

These are costs that change in line with output. Raw materials for production, packaging materials, bonuses, piece rates, sales commission and postage are some examples. The important characteristic of a variable cost is that it rises or falls in direct proportion to any growth or decline in output volumes.

There is a popular misconception that fixed costs are those costs that are predictable, and variable costs are those that are subject to change at any moment. The definitions already given are the only valid ones for costing purposes.

Semi-variable costs

Unfortunately, not all costs fit easily into either the fixed or variable category. Some costs have both a fixed and a variable element. For example, telephone services often have a monthly or quarterly rental cost that is fixed, and a cost per unit consumed, which is variable. In this particular example low-usage consumers can be seriously penalized. If only a few calls are made each month, the total cost per call (fixed rental + cost per unit, all divided by the number of calls) can be quite expensive.

Other examples of this dual-component cost are photocopier rentals, electricity and gas. These semi-variable costs must be split into their fixed and variable elements. For most businesses this will be a fairly simple process; nevertheless, it is essential to do it accurately or else much of the purpose and benefits of this method of cost analysis will be wasted.

The dynamic behaviour of costs

Now we can bring both these different types of cost together and see how they behave (see Figure 1.1). The horizontal line shows a static level of fixed costs over a particular range of output, say the rent of a premises. The variable costs are incurred in addition to the fixed costs and so start from the plateau line that represents the level of those fixed costs. This in turn produces a line showing the total costs. Taking vertical and horizontal lines from any point in the total cost line will give the total costs for any chosen output volume. This is an essential feature of the costing model that lets us see how costs change with different output volumes: in other words, accommodating the dynamic nature of a business.

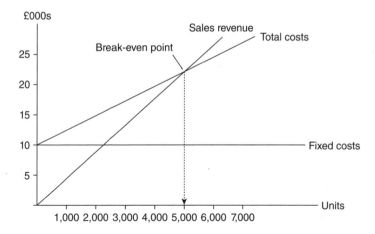

Figure 1.1 The costing model

It is to be hoped that we are not simply producing things and creating costs. We are also selling things and creating income. So a further line can be added to the model to show sales revenue as it comes in.

The point where the sales revenue line crosses the total costs line is the break-even point (BEP). It is only after that point has been reached that a business can start to make a profit. We can work this out by drawing a graph, such as the example in Figure 1.1, or by using a simple formula. To help bring the model to life, let's add some figures, for illustration purposes only.

The advantage of using the formula as well is that you can experiment by changing the values of some of the elements in the model quickly.

The equation for the BEP is:

$$\text{Break-even point} = \text{fixed costs} / (\text{Unit selling price} - \text{unit variable costs})$$

This is quite logical. Before you can reach profits you must pay for the variable costs. This is done by deducting those costs from the unit selling price. What is left (usually called the unit contribution) is available to meet the fixed costs. Once enough units have been sold to meet these fixed costs, the BEP has been reached.

The costs to be cut

With the nature of costs in mind we can see that two very different types of costs arise and that tackling them affects different aspects of business performance:

- Fixed costs: the fewer of these we have, the less we have to sell to reach any given level of profit.
- Unit variable costs: the lower these are at any given selling price, the higher the contribution and hence the sooner we pass the break-even point and start making profit.

Although we can't really consider the selling price of a product or service as a cost, it is part of the costing equation and as such it is an area we will explore as part of cost cutting.

Cutting costs is always done with an objective in view. Ultimately that objective can always be traced back to making the business a better one. But what exactly constitutes better? Bigger premises, more staff, increased market share, higher profits? All these may be desirable but lack a degree of permanence and precision, useful features of any enduring task such as cost cutting. Suppose you were looking to put some money into a bank or government security and to eliminate any unnecessary distractions, let's assume it is relatively risk free (if such a thing exists when you come to read this chapter). The yardstick against which you would assess one such investment against another would always include the interest rate. All things being equal, a return of 10 per cent on your cash would be better than one of 5 per cent.

In business, return on assets, or to use its more common title, return on investment (ROI), is the enduring measure that tells you if your performance is getting better over time, or is better or worse than a competitor's. Look at Table 1.3 below.

Table 1.3 Factors that affect profit performance

	£/$/€		£/$/€
Sales	100,000	Fixed assets	12,500
– cost of sales	50,000		
= gross profit	50,000	Working capital:	
– expenses	33,000	current assets	23,100
= operating profit	17,000	– current liabilities	6,690
– finance charges	8,090	=	16,410
= net profit	8,910	Total net assets	28,910

You can see the above table is nothing more than a simplified profit and loss account on the left, and the assets section of the balance sheet showing the capital employed on the right. Any change that increases net profit (more sales, lower expenses, less tax, etc) but does not increase the amount of assets employed (lower stocks, fewer debtors, etc) will increase the return on assets. Conversely, any change that increases capital employed without increasing profits in proportion will reduce the return on assets.

Now let us suppose that events occur to increase sales by 25,000 and profits by 1,000 to 8,910. Superficially that would look like an improved position. But if we then discover that in order to achieve that extra profit new equipment costing 5,000 was required and a further 2,500 had to be tied up in working capital (stock and debtors), the picture might not look so attractive. The return being made on assets employed has dropped from 31 per cent (8,910/28,910 × 100) to 27 per cent (9,910/[28,910 + 5,000 + 2,500] × 100).

The purpose of cost cutting is to ensure that the organization makes a satisfactory profit, enough to keep attracting investors; is prudently run, so has a good chance of surviving when the going gets tough; and is able to take advantage of growth opportunities.

Using the ROI framework for reviewing costs

In the next six chapters we will analyse and evaluate the range of cost-cutting strategies open to any organization using the ROI as our framework. The strength in taking this approach is that the balance sheet that contains the seeds of most fixed costs and the profit and loss account that houses most of the variable costs are documents common to all businesses. As such these reports can be used to help identify where costs are getting out of line in relation to the overall performance and as a budgeting framework to set cost-cutting goals.

Just having the balance sheet and profit and loss account of a business is not of much use in itself if you can't analyse and interpret the data. The tools for measuring the relationship between various elements of performance to see whether we are getting better or worse are known as ratios; simply put, these involve expressing one thing as a proportion of another with a view to gaining an appreciation of what has happened. For example, miles per gallon is a measure of the efficiency of a motor vehicle. If that ratio is 40 mpg in one period and 30 mpg in another, it would be a cause for concern and investigation as to what had caused the drop in performance.

A comparable business example could involve, say, looking at the cost of buying in materials and of manufacturing labour. Just knowing that those costs had doubled from, say, 100,000 to 200,000 from one period to another is of little value until you relate it to the level of business activity. So if sales have at least doubled whilst costs have 'gone up', they are actually in line with expectations. If sales have more than doubled, costs have actually dropped on a money value of sales basis, much as if your motor vehicle had used more fuel because more miles were travelled, but mpg had improved.

Ratios are used to compare cost performance in one period, say last month or year, with another – this month or year: they can also be used to see how well your business is performing compared with another, say a competitor's. You can also use ratios to compare how well you have done against your target or budget. In the financial field the opportunity for calculating ratios is great; but for computing useful ratios, it is not quite so great. The appropriate ratios are used in each of the following chapters.

Three more facts about costs

Costs may seem to fit squarely into the boring area of management. Unlike, say, leadership, team building, rewards, share options, mergers and acquisitions or Web 2.0 marketing (57 million entries on Google), cost cutting seems boring and mundane. Essential, perhaps, but costs and cutting them are hardly activities that are likely to lead to an adrenalin surge. Experienced cost managers will know that nothing could be further from the truth. There are three facts about costs, aside from their nature and how to analyse them that the CCCO should appreciate, that will make the subject both more fun and more rewarding.

Cost leadership is a desirable strategic goal in itself

Credit for devising the most succinct and usable way to get a handle on the big picture on the subject of cost has to be given to Michael E Porter of Harvard Business School, who trained as an economist at Princeton. His book, *Competitive Strategy: Techniques for Analyzing Industries and Competitors* (Free Press, Old Tappan, New Jersey, USA, 1980), is essential reading in most business schools. Porter observed that two factors above all influenced a business's chances of making superior profits. First, there was the attractiveness or otherwise of the industry in which it primarily operated. Second, and in terms of an organization's sphere of influence more important, was how the business positions itself within that industry. In that respect a business could only have a cost advantage in that it could make a product or deliver a service for less than others. Or it could be different in a way that mattered to consumers, so that the business's offering would be unique, or at least relatively so. Porter added a further twist to his prescription. Businesses could follow either a cost-advantage path or a differentiation path industry wide, or they could take a third path – they could concentrate on a narrow specific segment either with cost advantage or differentiation. This he termed 'focus' strategy.

Cost leadership is not the same as low price (or even low quality)

Low cost should not be confused with low price. A business with low costs may or may not pass those savings on to customers.

Alternatively, they could use that position alongside tight cost controls and low margins to create an effective barrier to others who might be considering either entering or extending their penetration of that market. Low-cost strategies are most likely to be achievable in large markets, requiring large-scale capital investment, where production or service volumes are high and economies of scale can be achieved from long runs.

Low costs are not a lucky accident

Low costs can be achieved through these main activities:

- Operating efficiencies: new processes and methods of working or less costly ways of working. Ryanair and easyJet are examples where analysing every component of the business made it possible to strip out major elements of cost: meals, free baggage and allocated seating, for example, whilst leaving the essential proposition – We will fly you from A to B – intact. British Airways, in contrast, has a very different strategy and different cost base to match.
- Product redesign: this involves rethinking a product or service proposition fundamentally to look for more efficient ways to work, or cheaper substitute materials to work with. The motor industry has adopted this approach with 'platform sharing', that is, where major players including Citroën, Peugeot and Toyota have rethought their entry models to share major components.
- Product standardization: a wide range of product and service offers claiming to extend customer choice invariably leads to higher costs. The challenge is to be sure that proliferation gives real choice and adds value. In 2008 the UK railway network took a long hard look at its dozens of different fare structures and scores of names, often for identical price structures, that had remained largely unchanged since the 1960s, and reduced them to three basic product propositions. Adopting this and other common standards across the rail

network is estimated to substantially reduce the currently excessive £500 million ($826 million) transaction cost of selling £5 billion ($8.26 billion) worth of tickets.

- Economies of scale: these can be achieved only by being big or bold. The same head office, warehousing network and distribution chain can support Tesco's 3,263 stores as it can, say, the 997 that Somerfield have. The former will have a lower cost base by virtue of having more outlets to spread its costs over as well as having more purchasing power.

All these areas and more will be examined in the chapters that follow.

IKEA

Furniture company IKEA was founded by Ingvar Kamprad when he was just 17, having cut his teeth on selling matches to his nearby neighbours at the age of five, followed by a spell selling flower seeds, greeting cards, Christmas decorations and eventually furniture. IKEA targets young white-collar workers as its prime customer segment, selling through 235 stores in more than 30 countries. Kamprad, an entrepreneur from Småland province in southern Sweden, offers home furnishing products of good function and design at prices young people can afford. He achieves this by using simple cost-cutting solutions that do not affect the quality of the products.

Worth £16 billion ($26.43 billion), Kamprad is the world's seventh-richest man but lives frugally, in keeping with the no-nonsense functional nature of the IKEA brand. He lives in a bungalow, flies easyJet and drives a 15-year-old Volvo. When he arrived at a gala dinner recently to collect a business award, the security guard turned him away because they saw him getting off a bus. He and his wife Margaretha are often seen dining in cheap restaurants. He does his food shopping in the afternoon when prices are lower and even then haggles prices down.

The experience (or learning) curve

The fact that costs declined as the output volume of a product or service increased, though well known earlier, was first developed as a usable accounting process by T P Wright, a US aeronautical engineer, in 1936. His process became known as the cumulative average model or Wright's model. Subsequent models were developed by a team of researchers at Stanford; these were known as unit time models or Crawford's models. The Boston Consulting Group (BCG) popularized the process with their experience curve, showing that each time the cumulative volume of doing something – either making a product or delivering a service – doubled, the unit cost dropped by a constant and predictable amount. The reasons for the cost drop include:

■ Repetition makes people more familiar with tasks and consequently faster.
■ More efficient materials and equipment become available from suppliers themselves as their costs go down through the experience curve effect.
■ Organization, management and control procedures improve.
■ Engineering and production problems are solved.

The value of the experience curve as a strategic process is that it helps a business predict future unit costs and gives a signal when costs fail to drop at the historical rate, both vital pieces of information for firms pursuing a cost-leadership strategy. Every industry has a different experience curve that itself varies over time (see Figure 1.2). You can find out more about how to calculate the curve for your industry on the Management and Accounting website (http://maaw.info/LearningCurveSummary.htm); the National Aeronautics and Space Agency (http://cost.jsc.nasa.gov/learn.html) provides a learning curve calculator.

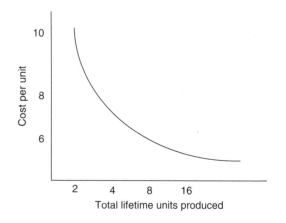

Figure 1.2 The experience curve

Pareto's 80/20 rule

Costs that may have quite properly and reasonably been incurred invariably over time become misallocated or unfairly distributed. In 1906, Italian economist Vilfredo Pareto used a formula to describe the unequal distribution of wealth in his country, after noting that 20 per cent of the people owned 80 per cent of the wealth. Others recognized the same relationship in their own areas of expertise, including quality and cost management pioneer Dr Joseph Juran, who called the subject 'the vital few and trivial many'. Pareto's Principle is more widely known and understood as the 80/20 rule, which states that 80 per cent of effort goes into producing 20 per cent of the results. Look at Table 1.4, which is a real example showing the number of customers a salesperson had, the value of his sales and the value of his potential sales. This more or less confirms the rule, as 18 per cent of customers account for 78 per cent of sales.

Interestingly enough, when the salesman in the above example was asked where he thought his sales in two years' time would be coming from (see last column in the table), he felt that his top 18 per cent of customers would account for 88 per cent of sales (up from 78 per cent of actual sales this year).

Table 1.4 The misallocated sales cost

Number of customers		Value of actual sales		Value of sales potential	
	%	000	%	000	%
4	3	710	69	1,200	71
21	18	800	78	1,500	88
47	41	918	90	1,600	94
116	100	1,025	100	1,700	100

An analysis of this salesman's call reports showed that over 60 per cent of time was spent calling on the bottom 68 accounts, and he planned to continue doing so. As these customers accounted for little more than 10 per cent of sales, time was being seriously misallocated. As the salesperson expected that the top 25 accounts would account for most of future growth, this misallocation of resource was scheduled to get worse. This activity-based rather than results-based outlook was being used by the sales manager to make out a case for an additional salesperson. What was actually needed was a call-grading system to lower the call rate on accounts with the least sales potential. So, for example, accounts with the least potential were called on twice a year and phoned twice, whilst top-grade accounts were visited up to eight times a year. When introduced, the grading process saved costs, eliminated the need for an additional salesperson and freed up time so the salesman could prospect for new, high-potential accounts.

The 80/20 rule can be used across all areas of a business to uncover other areas where costs are being incurred that are unwarranted by the benefits. In some areas you just need to open your eyes to see waste, which is what the rest of this book is intended to help with.

Cost-cutting assignment 1

Don't worry too much if this assignment looks more like getting a handle on costs than on ways to trim them. Be patient – there will be enough of that in the next chapters. For now the most important task is to be sure you understand your costs, where they are and how you stack up against other players in the market.

1 Work through your profit and loss account and calculate the margins for gross profit, operating profit and net profit for the past three years. Are these improving or deteriorating? Can you explain the changes? Get your accountant to help if you are not completely comfortable and/or read my book, *Practical Financial Management* (Kogan Page, 2008).

2 Now do the same for your three main competitors and assess your performance compared with theirs. (See Chapter 9 for more on benchmarking).

3 Where does your company fit in the cost matrix in Figure 1.3? This is not an exact science by any means. However, based on your knowledge of the market, an appreciation of how important cost is to your key customers (look back to the Ryanair vs British Airways example above) and your assessment of relative costs from the accounts, have a shot at positioning your business and your competitors on the matrix. It will give you some idea of the scope of the cost-cutting activity that lies ahead.

4 Take any easily measurable activity in your business – for example, the proportion of customers or products that account for over 80 per cent of sales (or better still, profits, if you can get at the figures). Then see how much resource or cost is tied up in that area compared with the part of the business that makes the least profit or delivers the least sales. The more out of balance the figures are, the greater the scope there is for cost cutting.

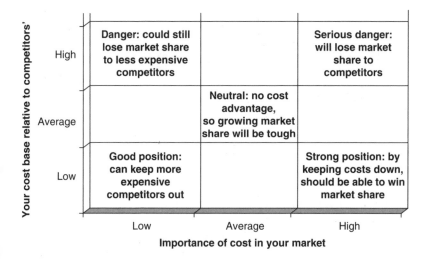

Figure 1.3 Assessing your strategic cost position

2
Kill Bill I: reduce capital expenditure

- Understanding cash costs;
- Totting up space requirements;
- Getting property costs down;
- Trimming back on equipment costs;
- Outsourcing – everything and anything;
- Monitoring value on capital expenditure.

For most businesses, but not all, capital expenditure is the big killer when it comes to cost. Premises, computers, equipment and the like eat up more than half of a business's expenditure on average and sometimes a good bit more. The problem from the CCCO's perspective is that capital expenditure has a long tail and what you see as an expense on the profit and loss account occurred sometime in the past, and there is no point trying to set challenging targets to cut costs that have already occurred.

For non-accountants we will need to make a short excursion into the arcane way in which capital costs show up in the accounts.

Cut cash costs, not depreciation costs

Accounting reports always assume that a business will continue trading indefinitely into the future – unless there is good evidence to the contrary. This concept is known in the trade as a 'going concern'. This means that the assets of the business are looked at simply as profit generators and not as being available for sale themselves and so creating a profit or loss on disposal. That in turn means that assets are usually entered into the accounts at their cost at date of purchase. For a variety of reasons, the real 'worth' of an asset will probably change over time. The worth, or value, of an asset is a subjective estimate on which no two people are likely to agree. This is made even more complex, and artificial, because the assets themselves are usually not for sale.

So in the search for objectivity, the accountants have settled for cost as the figure to record. It does mean that a balance sheet does not show the current worth or value of a business or the underlying assets. That is not its intention. Nor does it mean that the 'cost' figure remains unchanged forever. For example, a motor vehicle costing £6,000 ($9,912) may end up looking like this (Table 2. 1) after two years:

Table 2.1 Example of the changing worth of an asset

Year 1		Year 2	
	£/$/€		£/$/€
Fixed assets:		Fixed assets:	
Vehicle	6,000	Vehicle	6,000
Less depreciation	1,500	Less cumulative depreciation	3,000
Net asset	4,500	Net asset	3,000

The depreciation is how we show the asset being 'consumed' over its working life. It is simply a bookkeeping record to allow us to allocate some of the cost of an asset to the appropriate time period and enter that amount on the profit and loss account (income statement).

The time period will be determined by factors such as the working life of the asset. The tax authorities do not allow depreciation as a business expense, so this figure cannot be manipulated to reduce tax liability, for example. A tax relief on the capital expenditure known as 'writing down' is allowed, using a formula set by government that varies from time to time depending on its current economic goals, for example, to stimulate capital expenditure. We will look at opportunities for reducing costs in this area in Chapter 7.

Other assets, such as freehold land and buildings, will be revalued from time to time, which has a further effect on the rate of depreciation that shows up in the profit and loss account.

Depreciation distorts spending plans

Whilst depreciation is a valuable tool to help accounts apportion the cost of long-living assets over their working lives, it can distort the true cash cost of expenses and give false comfort to the CCCO. A declining rate of depreciation would suggest that costs overall were declining when in fact nothing material had changed. There are two reasons for this. In the first place, older assets will be fully depreciated, so will drop out of the figures. The assets themselves will still be there and be usefully employed, but their capital cost has been accounted for already. Second, a number of assets will be depreciated using the declining balance method. The example in Table 2.1 uses the straight-line method of depreciation, where the amount of depreciation is the same each year, whilst the declining-balance method takes a set percentage. So if the depreciation rate is set at 25 per cent of the declining balance in the example in Table 2.1, the first year's depreciation remains at 1,500 but for year two it drops to 1,125 (25 per cent of the written-down net asset value of 4,500).

Look at Table 2.2. The costs as shown in the profit and loss account (income statement) have dropped slightly over the past year and look set to keep dropping for the next two years according to plan: a satisfactory position, you might think. However, when we add back depreciation, which is after all the direct result of past capital expenditure decisions, and we are actually doing nothing now to reduce cost, the picture looks very different. The true cash costs are rising and when we add in the anticipated new capital expenditure the position deteriorates yet further. So though the profit and loss account may show costs are under

Table 2.2 Cash capital cost accounting

	Actual £/$/€		Projected £/$/€	
	Last year	This year	Next year	Year after that
Costs as per profit and loss account	100	99	98	96
Take out depreciation	(25)	(20)	(15)	(10)
True cash cost	75	79	83	86
Add new capital spend	25	30	35	40
Total cash cost	100	109	120	126

control and declining, this may well just reflect the impact of past capital expenditure decisions.

The past is truly another country when it comes to cost cutting. To scope the real position we need to recast the figures to show the true cash impact of capital expenditure decisions on future costs. In this not untypical example, costs appear to be being cut from 100 to 96 over the next two years, whilst they will actually be rising from 100 to 126 in real cash terms.

Sizing up space needs

For most organizations the premises from which they operate are the largest single cost area. The more space you take up, the higher the rent (or purchase price), and the more business rates are incurred. The other costs that are more or less directly related to your premises are insurance, heat, light and power, insurance, and repairs and maintenance. Location too plays an important part. Some businesses, for example, believe they have to locate in a prestige area either for reasons of image or to attract the best employees. The world's biggest international banks cling to Canary Wharf or Manhattan; 61 of the Fortune Global 500 companies are located in Tokyo, a city second only to London's West

End in occupancy costs. Often such beliefs are ill founded and simply result in a higher cost base for little or no tangible gain. Vodafone, the world's largest mobile phone company, kept its global headquarters in Newbury, some 60 miles to the west of London, for its first 20 years of operations. By doing so, the related overhead costs in terms of rents and salaries were a third lower than had they started out in London. Only in October 2009, when London office prices had dropped by 30 per cent and vacancy rates were up by 12 per cent did Vodafone move its global HQ to a new development in Paddington.

Work out what space you need and where you need it

Assessing how much space you really need is not rocket science. As a first step, make out a list of all the activities involved in getting your business to the point where it has something to sell. If you are going to run a bookkeeping service this could be quite a short list. You will need room for a desk, some filing cabinets and a computer. The Workplace (Health, Safety and Welfare) Regulations 1992, state that each employee should have 'sufficient floor area, height and unoccupied space for the purpose of health, safety and welfare'. Eleven cubic metres, ignoring any height above three metres, is the guideline for each worker, though this is a minimum and is dependent on other factors such as the amount of furniture and equipment to be used.

If you are going to manufacture, repair, assemble or process products, store and handle food, sell goods or services to the public at large, then a host of more complicated rules apply. It still doesn't have to be impossible to work out space needs. Tim Waterstone's first store, which opened in 1982, was, according to company history, based on a design produced by a student for less than £100.

You can use space-planning software such as SmartDraw (www.smartdraw.com>downloads), InstantPlanner (www.instantplanner.com) Autodesk (www.autodesk.com) or plan3D (www.plan3D.com), all of which have free or very low-cost tools for testing out your space layout. Or don't overlook the 'steam' method of laying cut-out models on paper. After all, Waterstone laid the foundations of a 320-store empire on nothing more complex (and incidentally, the company has an ongoing target to reduce floor space by 10 per cent a year).

Rent out spare space (and other services)

If you find after doing you space-needs calculation you have more space than you require, then you have three options. Stay put and suffer the extra cost burden: not an ideal choice. Move to smaller premises: whilst in the longer term you may save, in the short term you will have significant costs associated with moving as well as a level of disruption that will almost certainly reduce output. A better choice, as illustrated in the case study, would be to rent out your spare space. Atrium, the company in this example, managed to generate monthly cost savings that improved operating profits by around 12 per cent.

Atrium Ltd, founded by Patrick and Florence Dormoy, has operated from a showroom and office at London's Centrepoint, just off Tottenham Court Road, since 1986. Initially the business supplied retail dealerships with contemporary furniture and lighting sourced mainly from France, Belgium and Italy. The company's service extends to the delivery of the orders. This is facilitated through a 14,000 square foot warehouse in Park Royal owned by the company. There is a skilled delivery and installation team comprising five people based at this location.

The recession at the end of the 1980s saw a large proportion of the customer base of retail dealerships either go out of business or shift their focus from modern to traditional furniture. In response, Atrium shifted the strategic direction of the business to focus on the contract market, reached via the architecture and design community. Despite various changes in strategy, by 1997 it had become clear that the furniture side of the business that took the lion's share of space resources had little future. By concentrating on securing specifications from architects and designers and building strong long-term alliances with suppliers, Atrium built up annual sales to in excess of £6 million ($9.92 million) by 2009. Operating profits were in excess of £500,000 ($826,000).

A challenge for the company was how to make best use of its showroom, offices and warehouse, for which the new business had a much-reduced need. Four main cost-reduction strategies were pursued. The office area was converted to open plan, so allowing Atrium to free up sufficient space to lease an area to a supplier that required a London base for three of their staff. They also provided accounting services to this company, using their in-house management accountant. A mezzanine floor was built into the Park Royal warehouse, so providing a surplus that was rented out to a former competitor from the company's furniture-supply era. They also provided that company with a delivery and fitting service from their warehouse team.

Hot desking and teleworking

There are a couple of other options when it comes to freeing up space, either to allow you to grow without increasing the size of your premises or, like Atrium, to take advantage of space savings by renting that space to others. Either of these strategies will have the effect of reducing costs per unit of output.

Hot desking

Originating as a trend in the late 1980s to early 1990s, hot desking is defined as the temporary physical occupation of a workstation or desk area by a particular employee. The term seems likely to have come from the naval practice of hot racking, where sailors on different watches shared bunks. Hot desking can deliver considerable cost reduction through space savings – up to 30 per cent in some cases. Initially the technology to support the concept was either lacking or expensive. For example, 'follow me' phone systems where all you have to do is to dial in to your network, tap a few buttons and all calls to your company phone number will be redirected automatically to you, usually start at around £18,000 ($29,736) to £20,000 ($33,040) and are an add-on to your normal telephone system costs. But the near universal business use of mobile phones, widespread fast broadband and inexpensive netbooks has breathed life back into the idea.

Organizations as diverse as Coventry University, where 40 are involved in a hot-desk trial, or Procter & Gamble with hundreds of thousands of staff in 520 office/lab buildings dispersed across 160 countries are taking this approach. With 14 million square feet of office and research-centre space, it seemed obvious that Procter & Gamble could realize significant savings by increasing the occupancy levels of its buildings on a global basis. This task became increasingly urgent as the world economy hit the buffers in 2008. Workplace Services, a part of Procter & Gamble's global business services organization, specified the technologies to support work from any place, at any time, by any person, subject to a security profile. So far Procter & Gamble has achieved $20 million (£12.1 million) in annual cost savings from this project alone.

When Martin Stocks, managing director of Furniture For Business, wanted to expand his business he was faced with a seemingly insurmountable problem. His business, based in Putney (London), was set up to source and provide furniture for businesses, but without being tied to a single line of products so as to offer a more comprehensive and independent service. By 2004 the company had annual turnover of £9 million ($14.87 million) and had run out of space. Their location was ideal for Stocks and his two co-shareholders, was attractive to current and potential employees and was easily accessible to the architects and designers who specified their products. The last thing he wanted to do was to move the company and take on larger premises and run the risk of being left with a big overhead if the economy turned down and they had to slim down quickly.

Stocks needed to think a way around this because he had seen a number of businesses try and build themselves up followed by spectacular failure. He had office space for six in his sales team but needed to fit in ten. His solution was to provide each salesperson with a small trolley with space for their files, key literature and anything they might normally want on a desk. When they arrived at the office they took their trolley to a free desk, plugged their laptop in and started work. When they left for outside appointments, the activity that took up 60 per cent of their time, they cleared their desk, parked their trolley, leaving the desk area free for any new arrival.

Teleworking

This involves providing something akin to a hot desk, but in an outworker's home. Technology is not necessarily involved. Milkwood Publishing, for example, a small greeting-card business in West Cornwall, has a number of part-time workers who take home small pallets of around 5,000 cards to pick, pack and return each week. These complement the company's three-strong permanent team of packers, with the benefit that they don't occupy any space paid for by the business.

The internet, video conferencing, Skype, low-cost computing and worldwide same-day delivery services have made it possible for full- or part-time employees or contract workers to carry out a near-limitless range of activities off site. The advantages to the company using teleworkers include major cost savings on premises and such items as desks and chairs. It may also be able to draw on a wider range of employees, perhaps of a higher calibre, than would otherwise be the case. Milkwood, for example, has one outworker who could be in line to come in-house and supervise the whole packing operation.

Running the business from home

More than half of all new businesses start from home. Some never leave home and many others move back wholly or partially either when the going gets tough or when they recognize or rediscover the advantages. The benefits of operating from home include eliminating the daily travel grind and the stress associated with juggling home and business lives from different premises.

Less stress + more time = improved productivity. This is an equation that works for any business, but works best for a home-based one. It follows that if you can find a couple of extra hours a day you will get more done each day. The more valuable work you do, the more productive you are, and hence the more income you can generate. It's not rocket science. If you can make £20 ($33) an hour in your business, then every extra hour you work is to your advantage. Spend the four hours you might have spent travelling at productive work and you have an extra £80 ($132) a day. Do that five days a week for 48 weeks and you have an extra £19,200 ($30,462) of productive output. That makes a home-based business around a fifth more productive than the average business, with much lower costs per unit of output.

You'd be surprised just how much space can be found in and around the average family house and garden. Obvious areas such as a spare room or attic could provide between them anything up to 2,000 square feet and probably cost little more than the annual rent on the equivalent business premises. Going this route means that after the first year you are basically operating rent free. However, you will need to ensure you comply with local planning and building regulations, health and safety, insurance and the terms of your lease or mortgage.

Equipment efficiencies

Premises, though often the most costly area of fixed costs, are not always so, nor are they the only ones. People need vehicles, equipment, computers, desks and an ever-growing list of capital equipment to operate efficiently and to ensure that costs continue on a downward trend.

Production methods

In descending order of cost efficiency, the methods employed in making products pay are as follows. The cost per unit of output can be several times higher comparing batch production to lean manufacturing:

- One-off production is when a single product is made to the individual needs of a customer: for example, a designer dress. This is very much the pre-Adam Smith way in which everything was made, often without the use of any machinery.
- Batch production involves making a number of identical products at the same time, then moving on to make a different product later. For example, a small food-processing factory could make sausage rolls in the morning and pizzas in the afternoon. This approach requires some basic machinery and Smith would probably recognize this process were he alive today.
- Mass production is used for larger-scale production using machinery, often many different machines, for much of the work where individual tasks are carried out repetitively. This is an efficient and low-cost method of production for small and medium-sized businesses.
- Continuous-flow production produces the high volumes required by larger companies. These are highly automated and their cost usually requires them to be run 24/7. By reducing the manpower needed, this eliminates one of the blockages that Smith saw: 'The improvement of the dexterity of the workman necessarily increases the quantity of the work he can perform.'
- Computer-aided manufacture (CAM) is a continuous-flow production method controlled by computers, such as used in the motor industry.
- Lean manufacturing is an approach ascribed to Toyota, where they sought to eliminate or continuously reduce waste, defined as anything that doesn't add value. Waste in the production process taking the 'lean' approach is categorized under such headings as:
  - transport: keep processes close to each other to minimize movement;

- inventory: carrying high inventory levels costs money and, if too low, orders can be lost. 'Just in time' (JIT) manufacturing should be aimed for;
- motion: improve workplace ergonomics so as to maximize labour productivity;
- waiting: aim for a smooth, even flow so that workforce and machines are working optimally, reducing downtime to a minimum;
- defects: aim for zero defects, as that directly reduces the amount of waste.

If you are operating either of the first two production methods the chances of making a long-term success of serious cost cutting are low. Of course, if all your competitors use one-off or batch production you could still strive to be more efficient than them. But it may be better from a cost-cutting perspective at least to consider outsourcing (see below) to companies operating auto-mated and efficient production methods.

Getting equipped for less

If you do have to buy in either office furniture or equipment, there are plenty of sources offering good quality at a low cost. You should be able to fit out a basic office for around £50 ($83). For new furniture supplied to most European countries and around the world, check out Amazon.com (or the local Amazon website)>Home & Garden>Office or IKEA (www.ikea.com> then select your country>Workspace). In the UK, Habitat (www.habitat.net>United Kingdom>Products>Home office) also provide good-quality office products.

For second-hand office furniture, search Wantdontwant.com (www.wantdontwant.com), Green-Works (www.green-works. co.uk), who have outlets around the UK, and Office Furniture and Desks and Chairs (www.officefurnituredesksandchairs.co.uk). In the United States and Canada TRAS Office Solutions (www. trasoffice.com) claim to have the largest selection of used office furniture in North America. Tras obtains all its used goods from downsizings, bankruptcies and closures of all kinds at cents on the dollar.

For machinery and equipment you should use a trade magazine. Alternatively, in the UK, Friday-Ad (www.friday-ad.co.uk> For Sale>DIY & Tools), and Machinery Products UK (www.machineryproducts.co.uk) have second-hand machinery and tools of every description for sale. For the US market, Surplus Record (www.surplusrecord.com) provides an independent business directory of surplus, new and used machine tools, machinery and industrial equipment, listing over 60,000 items including metalworking and fabricating machine tools, chemical and process equipment, cranes, air compressors, pumps, motors, circuit breakers, generators, transformers, turbines, and more. Over 1,000 businesses list with Surplus Record. The directory is updated daily. Kitmondo (www.kitmondo.com) claims to be the internet's leading used-equipment marketplace, listing hundreds of categories of machines from abrasive planers to X-ray machines. Once you have selected the machinery or equipment you want, you can narrow the search by country or create an alert to let you know when a particular piece of second-hand equipment comes onto the market.

Comparing prices

There are over 200 price-comparison websites covering computer hardware and software, phones, travel, credit cards, bank accounts, loans, utilities, electrical goods, office products, including inkjet and printer supplies, and a few thousand more items a business might purchase. Paler.com, a quirky website run by Petru Palre (www.paler.com>UK Price Comparison Sites) has a directory listing these sites, with brief explanations and a helpful comments page where users have inserted more sites and additional information. There is a similar directory for international supplier comparison sites (www.paler.com>UK Price Comparison Sites> US/International). This is further split into United States and International.

Bartering online

You can avoid using up your cash by bartering your products and services for those of other businesses. Organizations that can help you get started with bartering include Bartercard (www.bartercard.co.uk; tel. 01276 415739), Barter Marketing (www.bartermarketing.com; tel. 0870 787 8100). Bartering is an international activity that is not confined to small businesses; more than 500,000 companies, including over half of the companies listed on the New York Stock Exchange, do in excess of $15 billion in barter annually. In the United States the International Reciprocal Trade Association (www.irta.com) provides a directory of B2B bartering associations (www.irta.com/Portals/0/SearchMembership.asp) covering the United States, Europe and a cross section of other countries including Brazil, Canada, New Zealand and Russia.

Hi-tech for less

Computers, the internet and communication systems in general have driven down the cost of almost every aspect of doing business. The cost base of every industry is directly affected by communications technology. Summit Research Associates, an American consultancy firm based in Rockville, Maryland, who regularly study the effects of technology on costs, claim that each self-service checkout replaces around 2.5 employees. If you ever wondered why your bank has so few staff in each branch, the answer lies in transaction costs. Retail banking costs $20 a transaction, telephone and postal banking brings the cost down to $5 and the internet takes that down again to 80 cents. Comverse.com, a provider of software systems for messaging and client management, aims to take customer-relationship cost cutting even further. Using their automated systems, the cost of dealing with queries can be reduced from $7 using a 'warm body' call centre to under 10 cents. One of their clients passes nearly a million calls a week through its online portal at a saving of over $50 million a year.

The cost of technology for IT and communications is now within the grasp of even the smallest business. That has opened up the global market to all, and to a certain extent levelled the playing field between big and small firms. But in doing so, technology has not only opened up distant markets that were once the prerogative of multinational goliaths, it has also made it easier for large firms to personalize their offers and compete in niche markets that were once too small and costly to be worth their while considering. Amazon and its subsidiary AbeBooks, for example, have cut a swathe through the world's second-hand bookshops, destroying the retirement aspirations of a million librarians in the process.

The following are areas to explore to get the most of the advantages of cost reducing technologies with significantly less cost.

Keep computer specifications down

Most businesses have seriously overspecified computers, spending on average 20 per cent more than is needed on unnecessary features. Outside the design and publishing fields there are few compelling reasons for having an Apple computer, costing a third more than the equivalent PC. Neither is there much point in having a PC capable of hosting an online gaming competition when your needs are confined to sending out invoices, e-mails and handling a basic website.

There is also a powerful argument for using laptops, certainly for anyone who is mobile or who could be moved to either a hot-desking or home-working basis (see sections above in this chapter). Certainly there are few valid reasons for anyone having both a desktop PC and a laptop, as there is virtually nothing that can't be done on either for much the same outlay.

To keep on top of what the latest specs and offers are, read PC World (www.pcworld.com>Hardware Reviews), CNET (www.cnet.com>Reviews) and IT Reviews (www.itreviews.co.uk). For Apple see the MacReviewZone (htpp://macreviewzone.com). You can keep abreast of developments in the laptop world at

Laptop Magazine (www.laptopmag.com>Reviews) and What Laptop (www.whatlaptop.co.uk).

Use free software

The most bought-in software licence used in business is Microsoft Office. For many businesses the money spent on making this suite of programmes available widely throughout the organization is a waste of money. There are free suites of programmes that will do much if not all of what most employees might require as well as meeting the general needs of most employees. Look into programmes such as OpenOffice (www.openoffice.org), whose free office programmes are compatible with Microsoft and work in some 30 languages; or Sun Microsystems (www.sun.com> Products>Software>Desktop>Office Productivity) whose Star Office 8 Writer priced at $69.95 claims to match Microsoft's product for small businesses but at one-fifth the cost.

Other free software sources include:

- Antivirus: a good free system that seems to work well is that from Grisoft (http://free.grisoft.com). Their AVG Anti-Virus Free edition provides basic protection but without any technical support.
- Business planning: Natwest Bank (http://www.natwest.com/global/business/day-to-day-business-planning-software.ashx) offers a free business-planning package for use on both PCs and Macs.
- Sofotex (www.sofotex.com): this is a portal to a wide range of freeware and shareware including programs for business functions, including accounting, bar-code software, contact management, invoicing, inventory management and project management.

Cloud computing

A recent survey of firms employing fewer than 250 people came up with the surprising result that for over a third of them, IT and related software were their biggest cost. One way round this cost is to hitch a ride on applications and pay only for the ride itself. Cloud computing is the generic name given to software hosted on the internet. You pay per use, so the upfront licence cost is eliminated, saving your company the time, money and hassle of managing IT solutions yourself. You have the added benefits of not having to buy updates, and though you have to be online to use the applications, that in turn means you can use them anywhere on any computer.

The range of software available on a cloud basis extends to customer-relations management (CRM), accounting, logistics, human-resource management, warehousing and fairly basic Office-type programs such as those provided by Google (docs. google.com), think free (www.thinkfree.com) and Ajax 13 (www. ajax13.com), all office suites that are compatible with Microsoft.

All this means that companies that a few years ago would have found it impossible to finance their start-up – yet alone grow into a global player in a few years – have a low-cost technology model at their fingertips. Twitter, which built its infrastructure on Amazon's E2 (cloud) platform, is living proof of how a small firm can get global reach for comparative peanuts.

Warren Bennett and David Hathiramani, co-founders and directors of A Suit That Fits.com are the first to admit that without access to cloud software their business would have found it hard to grow from a standing start three years ago to sales of £1.6 million ($2.64 million) in 2009. By reducing the classic tailored suit to a simple model, which allows customers to build the frills back up again, their online service keeps costs low without sacrificing quality. The suits are made in Nepal, sold online or via a mobile tailor service that they take around the country every few weeks or so.

All their software applications are online on a pay-per-use basis. Their calendars are run online, alongside production schedules and all product documentation. By having all software online they can literally operate all aspects of their business from any location and there are no big capital costs to hit them as they expand. The company now produces more bespoke suits annually than all of Savile Row, and the capital cost of their IT assets is less than for a conventional single-outlet retailer.

Outsourcing

One way to cut the cash costs associated with premises and equipment is to get others not on your payroll to do the work for you. That way they and their organizations provide the space, any machinery and even the staff. Outsourcing is the generic name for all the activity of contracting out the elements that are not considered absolutely core or central to the business. There are even occasions when firms use outsourcing when the product or service they are buying in is more expensive than using their own resources. For example, if buying a delivery vehicle costs £50,000 and together with a driver results in a cost per drop of £100 ($165.20), whilst using a delivery service costs £120 ($198.24), you would still be saving the capital costs. It would only be on the 2,500th delivery (50,000/20) that the extra costs became a cash burden.

There are obvious advantages to outsourcing aside from perhaps being the most significant and fertile area for cash cost savings touching almost very aspect of operations, as the next case study demonstrates.

The subject is of importance to companies of any size and the savings can be dramatic. For example, in 2008 IBM completed a major overhaul of its value chain and for the first time in its century-long history created an integrated supply chain (ISC) – a centralized worldwide approach to deciding what to do itself, what to buy in and where to buy in from. Suppliers were halved from 66,000 to 33,000; support locations were reduced from 300 to three global centres, Bangalore, Budapest and Shanghai. Manufacturing sites reduced from 15 to 9, all 'globally enabled' in that they can make almost any of the company's products at each plant and deliver them anywhere in the world. In the process IBM has lowered operating costs by more than $4 billion a year.

No manufacturing. No salesmen. No research and development. Jill Brown grew her business from a standing start to a turnover of £2 million ($3.31 million) a year in just five years as much by deciding what not to do as by what she actually does. The business she founded, Brown Electronics, supplies switches for computer equipment, the kind of gadget that, for example, allows half a dozen personal computers to use one printer between them.

She says: 'I didn't want to get into manufacturing myself, and I save myself the headaches. Why should I start manufacturing as long as I've got my bottom line right? Turnover is vanity, profit is sanity. I have worked for other people who wanted to grow big just for the kudos.'

Instead, Jill contracts out to other people's factories. She feels she still has control over quality, since any item that is not up to standard can be sent back. She also has the ultimate threat of taking away trade, which would leave the manufacturers she uses with a large void to fill. 'We would do so if quality was not good enough. Many manufacturers have underutilized capacity.'

Jill uses freelance salesmen on a commission basis. She explains: 'I didn't want a huge salesforce. Most sales managers sit in their cars at the side of the road filling in swindle sheets. Research and development is another area where expenses would be terrific. We have freelance design teams working on specific products. We give them a brief and they quote a price. The cost still works out at twice what you expected, but at least you have a measure of control. I could not afford to employ R&D staff full time and I would not need them full time. My system minimizes the risks and gives us a quality we could not afford as a small business.'

Indirectly, Jill provides work for about 380 people, whilst still being able to operate out of a space not much larger than a two-bedroom flat.

You can read up on the pros and cons of outsourcing, the sorts of activities a business can outsource, how to choose outsourcing partners and how to draw up a supply agreement with outsource suppliers at the Business Link website (www.businesslink.gov.uk> Grow your business>Growth through strategic outsourcing> Outsourcing).

Sunk costs

For a start-up venture or in cases where a new business or division is being created more or less from scratch, the cost savings from outsourcing are relatively easy to calculate. Subtract the cash costs of buying in from the cash cost of doing it yourself and if the number is positive, then you have a potentially viable strategy for reducing costs. You still need to check out the pros and cons above, but on the face of it, outsourcing could work.

The numbers are a bit trickier to arrive at if you are already carrying out the activity to be outsourced and have premises, equipment and people deployed in those areas. The concept we have to take on board here is that of sunk costs. These are money that you have already spent and that you won't get back, regardless of future outcomes. It's much like an annual fitness-club membership: the money is gone whether you go or not and there's no way to get it back. A good business example is Steve Job's ditching of Apple's Newton. The Newton was revolutionary, with great battery life, powerful handwriting recognition, and the NewtonOS operating system was state of the art. It was a forerunner of the PDA (personal digital assistant) and it had set the company back the best bit of $350 million (£212 million) by 1998. A previous CEO, John Scully, who got forced out because of poor stock performance, and two executives who left around the same time, Jean-Louis Gassée and Steve Sakoman, had championed the product. Jobs pulled the plug on the whole division that was developing it, taking the loss on the chin and arguing that it was a sunk cost and he had to move on to better investments.

Still, Jobs got off lightly compared to the US taxpayer who 'invested' some $121 billion (£73.32 billion) over two decades for an unserviceable fighter plane, the F-22. The government ploughed on, stating at a major review point: 'We've come this far; there's no turning back.' Once you have grasped the concept of sunk cost, you can turn back any time it makes economic sense to do so by ditching any emotional baggage. Jobs was lucky in so far as the Newton wasn't his baby, so he could close it down with no loss of face.

That sinking feeling

Look at Tables 2.3 and 2.4 below. They show the financial implications of operating a piece of equipment costing £90,000 ($148,680), used to frame prints. To keep things simple we will assume the equipment has no residual value and will not be usable after three years, but these factors don't affect this argument.

Table 2.3 Writing off the framer

	£			
Year	1	2	3	Total
Profit before depreciation	100,000	100,000	100,000	300,000
Less depreciation	0	0	0	0
Profit after depreciation	100,000	100,000	100,000	300,000
Loss from writing off equipment	90,000	0	0	90,000
Net profit	10,000	100,000	100,000	210,000

Table 2.4 Depreciating the framer

	£			
Year	1	2	3	Total
Profit before depreciation	100,000	100,000	100,000	300,000
Less depreciation	30,000	30,000	30,000	90,000
Net profit after depreciation	100,000	100,000	100,000	210,000

The company receives an offer to produce the frames for them at a price of £5 a frame, but the directors are reluctant to consider the offer as they have already invested heavily in the equipment. Are they right? The three-year profit will be the same whether they spread the cost over three years or take it in a single-year hit (ignoring the time value of cash, which we will be looking at in Chapter 9). So the book value of the equipment is irrelevant; the only factor to consider, all other things being equal, is whether the variable costs are lower.

The make-or-buy decision

Following on with this example, let's look in a bit more detail at trying to compute the possible savings from buying in the frames rather than making them. We expect to be able to make and sell 10,000 frames a year, using £20,000 ($33,040) of materials and £40,000 ($66,080) of labour, with no other costs involved. We have been offered a three-year fixed-supply contract at a price of £7 a unit, some £70,000 ($115,640) for the 10,000 frames. The traditional approach, ignoring depreciation as being a sunk cost, is set out in Table 2.5.

Table 2.5 The relevant costs (short term)

	£
Materials	20,000
Labour	40,000
Depreciation (sunk)	0
Total relevant costs	60,000
Less cost of contract	70,000
Net financial benefit	(10,000)

So in this case subcontracting would make us £10,000 worse off than continuing our own manufacturing. Clearly, if we could negotiate down to below £60,000 it would be worth considering.

Taking the long view

In the above example we would reject the decision and continue with manufacturing the frames ourselves and may well still have made the wrong decision. Over the long term we would have to replace the framer machine. By including the depreciation cost we end up with a very different sum (see Table 2.6).

Table 2.6 The relevant costs (long term)

	£
Materials	20,000
Labour	40,000
Depreciation (sunk)	30,000
Total relevant costs	90,000
Less cost of contract	70,000
Net financial benefit	20,000

If we extend our planning horizon to the indefinite future, then in this example we would be better off not doing the manufacturing ourselves. The optimal decision would be to either get the contract price down further or delay buying in for a year or two until we have had some benefit from buying in the framer. In any event, just because you made a poor decision in the past and produced in-house is no reason to perpetuate the error.

Tracking capital costs

Clearly, no business that hopes to have a long-term future can eliminate all capital expenditure. That would simply not be possible, as old equipment wears or becomes less productive than that of competitors. The only time when it may make good business sense to freeze all capital costs is when survival is the only thing that matters (see Chapter 8 for more on cutting costs in a crisis).

What you can do is keep these costs within a defined budget (see Chapter 9 for more on budgets) and apply a quick reality check as you go along. Look at Table 2.7, which shows how investment in fixed assets has changed or is planned to change between two periods. Below that figure are the sales and profit figures for the same time period.

Table 2.7 Capital costs: taking a reality check

	This period £/$/€	Last period £/$/€	Change %
Fixed assets	250,000	180,000	38.89
Sales turnover	5,000,000	4,000,000	25.0
Profit	600,000	500,000	20.0
Sales:fixed assets ratio	20:1	22.22:1	
Profit:fixed assets ratio	2.4:1	2.78:1	

One way we can see if we look like getting value out of capital costs is to calculate the percentage change in these three key figures. We can see in this example that investment in fixed assets is up by 38.89 per cent, whilst turnover and profits are up by a much smaller 25 per cent and 20 per cent respectively. Another way to show the position is to calculate the number of pounds or dollars of sales turnover and profit created by one pound or dollar spent in fixed assets. We can see here that every pound or dollar in fixed assets yielded 20 of sales and 2.4 of profit this period, a worse performance than last period when the figures where 22.22 and 2.78 respectively. Either way of tracking is fine, but often managers can relate better to a number than a percentage.

Starbucks

Most people believe Howard Schultz to be the founder of Starbucks, but that accolade belongs to Jerry Baldwin, Zev Siegl and Gordon Bowker, three friends who shared a passion for fresh coffee. They opened their first outlet in Seattle in 1971 and by the time Shultz, a plastics salesman for Hammarplast, saw the opportunity to roll the business out, it was 1981 and Starbucks was the largest business in Washington, with six retail outlets selling fresh coffee beans. Shultz's vision was to create community gathering places like the great coffee houses of Italy and transplant them to the United States.

The idea didn't strike a cord with Baldwin, who had hired Shultz in as his marketing manager, but he let him try out the concept of selling espresso by the cup in one of his stores. Baldwin remained unconvinced, so Shultz started out on his own, opening a coffee house he named Il Giornale, after Italy's then biggest-selling newspaper.

In 1987 the owners of Starbucks wanted to sell out, and Schultz convinced a group of local investors to stump up $3.7 million (£2.22 million) with the goal of opening 125 outlets over the following five years. Shultz abandoned the name Il Giornale in favour of Starbucks and has gone on to open more than 15,000 retail locations in North America, Latin America, Europe, the Middle East and the Pacific Rim.

Starbucks don't just open outlets, they close them too. When a lease comes up for renewal, or sales dip, the outlet's viability is reviewed. Sometimes it's the customers who have moved away and sometimes rents are out of line. Globally, Starbucks launched a programme in September 2009 to slash costs by $500 million (£306 million), which involved selling or agreeing lower rents in around 50 loss-making stores in the UK alone.

Cost-cutting assignment 2

When tackling these assignments it's important to remember it is only future cash costs that you can influence. Depreciation costs may well be one of the biggest cost numbers in your accounts but those costs are all sunk (look back to earlier in this chapter if you are still a little hazy on the subject of sunk costs and depreciation).

1 Assess how much space you really need to run your business. Then check out how much space you now have. If you have more space than you need (don't forget that height and some outside areas can be included here), then review your options for renting out surplus space in the short term and perhaps moving to smaller premises in the longer term.

2 If you have too little space or are likely to need more in the future, then check out all the options for keeping property

costs in check. Do all your workers have to work on your premises? Is there scope for hot desking or teleworking?

3   Have you bought equipment, computers and software at the best-possible prices?

4   Do you have to do everything you are currently involved in or could some, perhaps even most, of the capital-intensive activities – particularly concerning premises and equipment – be outsourced? That would move future capital costs out of your books altogether.

5   How do your capital costs per pound or dollar of sales and profit stack up against an earlier period and those of your competitors? (See Chapter 9 for more on benchmarking.)

3

Kill Bill II: make working capital work

- Understanding working capital;
- Cutting stock and inventory levels;
- Getting customers to pay up;
- Collaborating with suppliers;
- Recognizing cost drift warning signs.

Every bit as important as the money tied up in fixed assets is the shorter-term cash revolving around the business in working capital. This is much more difficult to control than fixed assets as actions such as buying a new computer or a piece of machinery tend to be infrequent and considered decisions. Letting stocks and work in progress build up and allowing customers a bit more leeway with their payments are subject to mission creep. Bit by bit as a business grows, discipline slips and working capital grows, with the result that profitability declines. Having a bigger business that is less profitable is not a route to enhanced value.

Table 3.1 shows a simplified set of accounts for the working capital and turnover of a business for last year and this. It shows that whilst the sales have grown by 20 per cent, the amount of money tied up in working capital has increased by 51 per cent. If the company had controlled its working capital better it would have required only a further 92,000 (20 per cent of 460,000). Instead it has pumped 235,000 more into working capital. That in turn means more costs in terms of financing charges and space to carry additional stock. It has even become virtual bankers to its customers, lending them 300,000 interest free.

Table 3.1 Uncontrolled working capital when sales are rising

	Last year £/$/€ 000	This year £/$/€ 000
Current assets:		
Stock (product for sale)	500	700
Debtors (customers yet to pay up)	200	300
Cash on hand	10	5
	710	1,005
Less current liabilities:		
Creditors (people we owe money to)	250	260
Overdraft	0	50
	250	310
Net current assets or working capital (current assets – current liabilities)	460	695 (+51%)
Sales turnover	1,000	1,200 (+20%)

The cost problems in this example were masked by the fact that the business was growing. But when the going gets tough, things will look very different. To quote Warren Buffett: 'You only find out who is swimming naked when the tide goes out.' Table 3.2 shows what happened to Coffee Republic when their tide went out.

Whilst their sales collapsed by 40 per cent due in part to the economic slump, their use of current assets rose by 19 per cent, funded by taking extended credit from suppliers, an untenable long-term cost-reducing strategy. Unsurprisingly their auditors, BDO Stoy Hayward, include this sentence in the introduction to their accounts: 'There exist uncertainties which may cast doubt over the Group's ability to continue as a going concern.' Coffee Republic went bust in July 2009.

Table 3.2 Uncontrolled working capital when sales declined at Coffee Republic

	March 2007 $ 000	March 2008 $ 000
Sales turnover	9,719	5,849 (–40%)
Current assets:		
Stock (product for sale)	47	19 (–60%)
Debtors (customers yet to pay up)	1,054	1,247 (+18%)
Cash on hand	25	19
	1,079	1,285 (+19%)
Less current liabilities:		
Creditors (people they owed money to)	726	1,684 (+131%)

The working-capital cycle

Figure 3.1 shows the typical path of working capital through a business. We start out with cash, either our own or if we have run out short-term borrowings in the form of an overdraft from a bank. This money is used to buy in materials, which are worked up into finished goods to sell to customers. We pay our suppliers, get paid by our customers and end up with some cash (or an approved overdraft) to keep the cycle moving round.

The rest of this chapter is about ways to either keep as little money as possible tied up in working capital or speed up the rate at which working capital circulates, both key strategies in the CCCO's armoury.

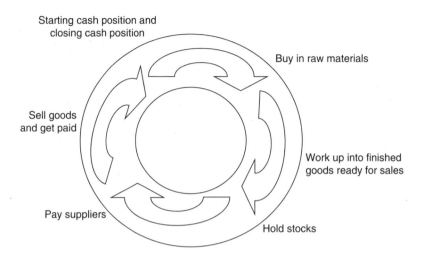

Starting cash position and closing cash position

Buy in raw materials

Sell goods and get paid

Work up into finished goods ready for sales

Pay suppliers

Hold stocks

Figure 3.1 The working-capital cycle

Fascia Graphics

Fascia Graphics Limited, based in Chippenham, was founded in 1994 by Paul Bennett. The company is a market leader in the production of membrane switches, membrane keyboards, graphic overlays, screen-printed labels, nameplates and associated products to quality standard BS EN ISO 9001:2000. It services a number of business sectors including medical, security and fire protection, supplying products to companies across Europe, the United States and Asia.

The company operates out of a 15,000 square foot factory employing 60 staff. Its products are bespoke and all the information needed to fulfil each order – specifications, plans, drawings, customer approval processes and a route card with manufacturing instructions – is contained in a job bag. In theory the job bag stays with the product as it moves through various stages of the manufacturing process. In practice any of the 17,000 or so job bags being used at any one time could be in any of half a dozen locations and be difficult to find quickly. Job bags have been known to take weeks to track down, though a few hours is a more typical timescale. Large amounts of time are wasted tracing job bags, and where they are lost for too long, artwork and other processes may have to be repeated. All in all this extends the production cycle significantly and the company has investigated ways to shorten this cycle and so reduce costs. The solution Fascia has come up is RFID (Radio Frequency Identification), a tag system that uses a wireless transceiver that can detect an item as small as a job bag to within a few feet. This will allow the company to speed up the production flow through the factory as well as monitor work in progress and finished-goods stock to maintain an optimum balance of each, all resulting in lower costs.

It's not just companies that can benefit from implementing working-capital efficiencies and cost-reduction strategies. The American Red Cross of Greater Cleveland (USA) received a Business Finance Vision award in 2007 for its success in implementing operations-efficiency measures. The organization helps people prepare and respond to disasters by providing a range of materials, books and training resources. Using Microsoft Dynamics, a software package that helps streamline warehouse, sales and operations, it has reduced staffing from 110 to 55 and cut stock holding by 50 per cent. Over the same period it has increased revenue from donors from $7.5 million (£4.54 million) to $9 million (£5.45 million). In the words of Richard Hankins, the Red Cross's CIO, 'We are doing more work and we are doing it smarter.'

Keeping stock costs down

High inventory levels are popular with marketing departments because having them makes satisfying customers an easier task; they are less popular with production departments, who have to carry inventory costs in their budgets. Finance departments insist on having the lowest-possible stock levels, as high stock pushes working capital levels up and return on investment down. (Look back to Chapter 1 to see how this works). This tussle between departments is a strategic issue that has to be resolved by top management. The birth of Waterstone's, the bookshop business founded by Tim Waterstone – fortuitously a marketing visionary, qualified accountant and the company's managing director –

provides an interesting illustration of the dimension of the stock-control issue. Until the advent of Waterstone's, the convention had been to store books spine out on shelves, in alphabetical order, and under major subject headings: computing, sport, travel, etc. This had the added advantage of making it easy to see what books needed reordering, and stock counts were a simple process. Waterstone, however, knew that 'browsers', the majority (60 per cent, according to his research) of people who go into bookshops to look around, had no idea what book they wanted, so didn't know where to start looking. His differentiating strategy was that as well as following the conventional model of having books on shelves, he scattered the books in piles around the store, using a variety of methods: new books in one pile, special offers in another. Sales and profits soared sufficiently to more than compensate for the near doubling of book stock.

But even where holding inventory is vital, it doesn't have to be held regardless of cost. Nicholas Piramal India Limited, one of India's largest and fastest-growing healthcare companies, has grown from 48th-largest to fourth-largest pharmaceutical manufacturer since first entering the pharmaceutical marketplace in 1988. With consolidated net sales of more than $300 million, they offer one of the broadest pharmaceutical portfolios in the country. Using a software program, i2 Factory Planner, they have brought material inventories down by 35 per cent, yielding more than $200,000 (£121,000) in annual interest cost savings whilst being able to meet customer demand in half a day rather than the two days taken previously. Where margins are tight, as in, say, the grocery field, keeping stock costs low and shrinking is key to profitability. For example, Wal-Mart's floor space devoted to holding stock is two and a half times smaller than the industry average.

Economic order quantity

Businesses have to carry a certain minimum amount of stock to ensure that the production pipeline works efficiently and likely demand is met. So the costs associated with ordering large quantities infrequently, thus reducing the order cost but increasing the cost of holding stock, has to be balanced with placing frequent orders, thereby pushing the costs in placing orders up but reducing stock-holding costs. Economic order quantity (EOQ) is basically an accounting formula that calculates the point at which the combination of order costs and inventory-carrying costs are least, so arriving at the most cost-effective quantity to order.

The formula for EOQ is:

$$\text{Economic order quantity} = \sqrt{(2 \times R \times O)/C}$$
where R = annual demand in units, O = cost of placing an order, C = cost of carrying a unit of inventory for the year.

InventoryOps.com, a website created and run by Dave Piasecki to support his book, *Inventory Accuracy: People, Processes, & Technology* (Ops Publishing, 2003), provides a useful starting point in your quest for information on all aspects of inventory management and warehouse operations. At this link (www.inventoryops.com/economic_order_quantity.htm), you will find a full explanation of how to use EOQ.

Amazon.com is a great example of superior stock management in action. Their business model fundamentally relies on fast-moving stock and even faster cash collection. Whilst stock is held in their warehouses an average of 19 days before being shipped to customers, payments are received just three days later through credit card purchases. The effect is that Amazon.com can ship product, get paid by customers, and even earn interest on the cash, before having to pay their suppliers.

Getting paid and paid faster

There are few faster and more certain areas to cut costs than in that surrounding debtors. When customers take credit, you are in effect bankrolling their business. When they take extended credit way beyond your usual trading terms, they are behaving much as someone who takes an unauthorized overdraft or breaches the level of their loan limit. But in these circumstances there are rarely any penalties. The biggest unnecessary cost of all is when a customer defaults on payment altogether, either because they have a gripe about quality or delivery or because they go bust.

If you are selling on credit and take 90 days to collect your money from customers (the average days' credit taken in 2009 was 89 days), then you are tying up an extra £150,000 ($150,000) cash for every £1 million ($1 million) of sales, compared to a firm that gets its money in 35 days. For a small firm with an annual turnover of around £3 million ($4.96 million), that could amount to the whole value of its overdraft. Looking at it another way, getting paid one week earlier would free up nearly £60,000 ($99,120) of cash and the interest that was being paid on it.

Chasing debtors

The most cost-effective and successful method of keeping late payers in line is to let them know you know. Nine out of 10 businesses do not routinely send out reminder letters advising customers that they have missed the payment date. Send out a polite reminder to arrive the day after payment is due, addressed to the person responsible for payments, which is almost invariably someone in the accounts department if you are dealing with a big organization. Follow this up within five days with a phone call, keeping the pressure up steadily until you are paid.

If you are polite and professional, consistently reminding them of your terms of trade, there is no reason why your relationship will be impaired. In any event, the person you sell too may not be the person you chase for payment.

If you still have difficulty, consider using a debt collection agency. You can find a directory of registered agents on the Credit Service Agency website (www.csa-uk.com/csa>Members list).

A very small amount of extra effort put in here can pay great dividends, and it's important to remember that the less cash needed to finance the business, the more profitable that business will be. Here are some other things you can do to get paid and paid faster:

- If you sell on credit, set our your terms of trade clearly on your invoices. Unless customers know when you expect to be paid, they will pay when it suits them.
- Ensure you meet delivery and quality requirements by getting customers to acknowledge receipt of goods and services, where possible.
- Find out when your biggest customers have their monthly cheque run and make sure your bills reach them in time.
- Always take trade references when giving credit and look at the customer's accounts to see how sound they are.
- Watch out for warning signs indicating that payment will be delayed or worse. These include: attempts to renegotiate terms of payment, broken promises on payment dates, deathly silence in which letters, statement of accounts, e-mails and chasing phone calls are ignored, and repeated requests for duplicates of invoices – which are usually just an attempt to stall and delay payment.
- Take out credit insurance on all major customers, typically the 20 per cent that account for 80 per cent of your business. If one of those fails to pay you could go under fast.

Credit cards

You can sidestep the whole business of getting cash in from customers by taking credit card payments. This may seem to go against the grain of cutting costs but it will make sure you have zero costs associated with bad debts or late collection. Those factors alone should produce cost savings, with the time and effort involved in not having to carry out credit checks, sending out statements and chasing up payment as an additional bonus. Getting paid by credit card makes it easier for customers to buy, and makes it certain that you will get your money almost immediately. With a merchant account, as the process of accepting cards is known, as long as you follow the rules and get authorization, the cash, less the card company's 1.5 to 3 per cent, gets to your bank account the day you charge.

You can get a merchant account without a trading history and operating from home, dependent of course on your credit record. Streamline (www.streamline.com), part of Royal Bank of Scotland, Barclaycard Merchant Service (www.barclaysmerchantservices. co.uk) and HSBC (www.hsbc.co.uk/1/2/business/home>Credit Card Processing) offer services in the field with set-up costs for a small business from around £150 ($247.80). They claim you can be up and running in a fortnight.

Resorting to law

If all else fails, it's important to make sure that customers know that in the last resort you will pursue them hard to get your money. Just remember, if you operate on a 20 per cent profit margin, for every customer that fails to pay you need to get five comparable orders in the bag from paying customers to make up lost ground.

There are a number of ways in which you can use the courts in a cost-effective manner to recover money owed.

The Small Claims Court offers a way for people whose claim is for relatively small sums (under £5,000), but would not be worth pursuing if you had to hire lawyers. Be warned, however, even if you win in the Small Claims Court you can still have problems enforcing the judgement and getting bad debtors to pay up. You can find information on the Small Claims Court at www.courtservice.gov.uk.

Fast Track is a route for claims between £5,000 and £15,000, or there is Multi Track for more complex cases and claims over £15,000. The rules on these are on the Lawpacks website at www.lawpack.co.uk/small_claims_faq.asp#4751).

Money Claim Online (www.moneyclaim.gov.uk/csmco2/index.jsp) is a service where those with claims of up to £100,000 can sue through the internet at any time, day or night. If the claim is undefended, the money can be recovered without anyone having to go to court.

Arbitration, which involves an independent person listening to the arguments of both sides and making a common-sense decision, is a less expensive, faster and less threatening way of getting disputes resolved. You have to agree to be bound by the decision and as with any other judgment, at the end of the day you still have to get the loser to pay up. But at least there is no dispute that the money is owed to you. The Chartered Institute of Arbitrators (www.arbitrators.org) and their European branch (www.european-arbitrators.org) have information on the arbitration process and a database of professional arbitrators.

Taking credit

If your customers take 90 days to pay up, it seems only fair that you should expect the same latitude from your suppliers. Normally the rule is to take credit from your suppliers up to the maximum time allowed. Going beyond that limit and becoming a 'bad payer' can leave you exposed to getting less than satisfactory service. You could even find that any cost savings made in this way are more than eliminated by the problems caused when your supplier ships late or holds back deliveries until you have settled all outstanding amounts.

But sometimes it may make good business sense to pay up promptly. Whilst this may sound insane, sometimes suppliers with cash-flow difficulties of their own offer what amount to excessively high rates of interest for settling up promptly.

Negotiate supplier discounts

If a supplier offers 2 per cent for payment in seven days rather than the 40 days they would usually allow, what is on offer is in effect 22.5 per cent equivalent interest. (Follow the steps in Table 3.3 to work out if prompt payment is a good investment.)

Table 3.3 Evaluating a discount offer

Step 1	Agree discount 2%
Step 2	100 – discount on offer = 98%
Step 3	Divide step 1 by step 2 = 0.020408
Step 4	Normal payment period in days = 40
Step 5	Payment period to get discount = 7 days
Step 6	Step 4 minus step 5 = 33
Step 7	365 divided by step 6 = 11.06061
Step 8	Step 7 × step 3 × 100 = 22.572%

So if that figure is higher than the return you are making in your own business, better than the cost of your borrowings from the bank, and if your cash flow can stand the pain, paying promptly may be a better way to reduce costs than many other options, particularly during a period of economic downturn. You can use the same arithmetic to work out what you can afford to pay out to get your money in earlier.

Ask for stock on consignment

In the supermarket grocery sector, where profit margins often are in single digits, companies such as Tesco, Sainsbury's and Morrison's have reduced order-to-delivery cycle times to fewer than four days on average and are aiming to reduce that further. One strategy being adopted here and in an increasing range of other sectors, particularly as a by-product of the credit crunch, is asking suppliers to hold materials for you as consignment stock. Suppliers then hold your materials in their warehouses, ideally close to your facilities, so that you can draw on them as and when required. Such materials are not formally purchased by you until the moment they are brought in for use and you can still negotiate supplier credit. This strategy has two major cost advantages. It cuts the cash cost of materials by shortening the working-capital cycle and it saves the cost of the space required for stock holding.

At first sight, consignment stock seems to be a strategy with only one winner, namely the company getting stock in this way. But to be truly successful and achieve enduring cost savings, there has to be something in it for both parties, as the Röhm and BASF Coatings case study shows.

BASF Coatings AG and Röhm GmbH & Co KG

BASF Coatings AG, a major paint supplier, and its relationship with Röhm GmbH & Co KG, an important supplier, is a case in point when it comes to holding stock on assignment. BASF can trace its roots back to 1903, when its parent company, Glasurit-Werke Max Winkelmann, started up in Münster-Hiltrup, Germany. With annual sales turnover of €2.5 billion (£2.2 billion, $3.63 billion) and strong market positions in Europe, North and South America, as well as the Asian Pacific region, and with satellite companies in Australia, China, India, Japan and the Philippines, the company has a complex supply and stock chain. The situation has been exacerbated by having the motor industry as a major customer segment, an industry that demands a high degree of flexibility from its suppliers and exerts strong cost pressure, never more so than during major economic downturns.

Initially Röhm and BASF Coatings maintained a fairly traditional customer–supplier relationship. At the beginning of each year BASF Coating would provide an approximate, non-binding estimate of requirements. Other than that no further information was provided, so production planning at Röhm was based almost entirely on past experience. The result was that both parties had problems. BASF experienced frequent stock shortages when demand accelerated and Röhm had idle capacity when the reverse occurred.

To overcome these supply problems, BASF Coatings initiated a project called PROGRESS (process integrated supply) and invited core suppliers, Röhm among them, to collaborate in order to reduce costs, shorten process and production times, and improve the quality of information and the level of service for all parties. As a result, Röhm now maintains consignment depots for BASF Coatings at BASF's plants, taking on tank fillings and deliveries on the basis of live online data on stock, forecasts and planned withdrawals submitted by BASF Coatings. BASF Coatings pays for the chemicals via credit (self-billing) as they are drawn off, with the relevant documentation delivered on a common electronic platform. BASF and Röhm calculated joint annual cost savings in excess of €500,000 (£439,000, $726,000).

Cash and overdrafts

Any unused money not tied up anywhere else in the business shows up in the cash balance in working capital, except where that money can be invested long term. Such long-term investments offer few opportunities for cost cutting and so fall outside the scope of this discussion. If a business gets paid quickly by its customers or better still is paid in cash, takes the maximum credit on offer and carries little stock, the chances are it will have a cash surplus. At certain times of the year, say when sales are sluggish and stocks high, a business may run out of cash and into the red. This will show up as an overdraft.

Although these areas fall into the working-capital arena, they are dealt with in Chapter 7, where the whole subject of minimizing financing costs is covered.

Keeping on top of working-capital costs

Here are some tools to help recognize cost-reduction opportunities in the area of working capital. The whole area is termed 'liquidity' and the measurements used to monitor it are known in the accounting field as 'tests'. These are the main relationships that provide a window into how efficiently working capital is being used and whether we are being prudent in terms of having sufficient short-term assets to meet short-term liabilities. Failing in the latter of these goals could more than offset any cost savings made. (Chapter 9 explains how to establish the sort of ratios a well-run business should be aiming for in your sector.)

Current ratio

Working capital as a figure alone doesn't tell us much. It is as if you knew your car had used 20 gallons of petrol but had no idea how far you had travelled. It would be more helpful to know how much larger the current assets are than the current liabilities. That would give us some idea if the funds would be available to pay bills for stock, cover tax liability and any other short-term liabilities that may arise. The current ratio, which is arrived at by dividing the current assets by the current liabilities, is the measure used. For the example shown in Table 3.1, the ratio for last year is $710/250 = 2.84$. The convention is to express this as 2.84:1 and the aim here is to have a ratio between 1.5:1 and 2:1. Any lower and bills can't be met easily; much higher and money is being tied up unnecessarily. So the ratio in Table 3.1 is high, showing that too much money is tied up in working capital and there should be plenty of opportunities for reducing costs. For the current year, the picture is rather worse, as the ratio has advanced to 3.24:1 (1005/310).

Quick ratio (acid test)

This is a belt-and-braces ratio used to ensure that a business has sufficient ready cash or near cash to meet all its current liabilities. Items such as stock are stripped out as although these are assets, the money involved is not immediately available to pay bills. In effect the only liquid assets a business has are cash, debtors and any short-term investment such as bank deposits or government securities. For our example this ratio is $210/250 = 0.84$:1 last year and a more healthy 0.98:1 (305/310) this year. The ratio should be greater than 1:1 for a business to be sufficiently liquid.

Average collection period

We can see in our example that the current ratio is high, which is an indication that some elements of working capital are being used inefficiently. The business has £200,000 ($330,400) owed by customers on sales of £1,000,000 ($1,652,000) over the year. The average period it takes to collect money owed is calculated by dividing the sales made on credit by the money owed (debtors) and multiplying it by the time period in days; in this case the sum is: 200,000/1,000,000 × 365 = 73 days. For the current year the collection period looks likely to extend to 91 days (300,000/1,200,000 × 365).

If the credit terms are net 30 days, then something is going seriously wrong. In this example it has been assumed that all the sales were made on credit.

Average payment period

This ratio shows how long a company is taking on average to pay its suppliers. The calculation is as for average collection period, but substituting creditors for debtors and purchase for sales.

Days' stock held

The business in our example is carrying £500,000 ($826,000) stock and over the period it sold £500,000 of stock at cost (the cost of sales is £500,000 to support £1,000,000 of invoiced sales, as the mark-up in this case is assumed to be 100 per cent). Using a similar sum as for the average collection period, we can calculate that the stock being held is sufficient to support 365 days' sales (500,000/500,000 × 365). Cutting stock back from 52 weeks to 13 would trim 182 days or £250,000 ($413,000) worth of stock out of working capital, saving £15,000 ($24,780) a year in interest costs (at 6 per cent), to say nothing of the saving in space to hold the stock. (Look back to Chapter 2 to see how to turn this space into cash and so lower property costs.)

Circulation of working capital

This is a measure used to evaluate the overall efficiency with which working capital is being used, that is, the sales divided by the working capital (current assets – current liabilities). In this example that sum is: 1,000,000/460,000 = 1.54 times. In other words, we are turning over the working capital more than one and a half times each year. There are no hard and fast rules as to what is an acceptable ratio. Clearly, the more times working capital is turned over, stock sold for example, the more chance a business has to make a profit on that activity.

Cost-cutting assignment 3

Go back over this chapter and look for ways to cut the costs associated with using working capital:

1 Calculate your current ratio for the past three years. Is it rising, showing that you are tying up more money in working capital and so taking on more costs, or is the position improving?
2 Now do the same sum for the best-performing company in your sector and see how you compare.
3 Work out the ratios for the other five liquidity tests above for each of your past three years and do the same for the best-performing company in your sector.
4 What are the key differences in performance between your business and the best company in the sector and that of your recent past? Do these figure reveal opportunities for cost cutting, eg reducing stock levels or collecting cash from customers faster, paying suppliers more slowly (or faster if the settlement discount is right)?
5 Are there ways in which we use our working capital in terms of production/operating processes that could be changed to improve work flow and reduce costs? (Look back to the Fascia Graphics and Nicholas Piramal cases for some pointers here.)

4
Max up margins

- Motivate for margin;
- Remove loss makers;
- Buy better;
- Sell to the right market;
- Stop waste and fraud.

Some of the most important figures in the whole field of cost management are those that are included in calculating gross profit. Whatever our activity, we have to buy certain raw materials. These include anything you have to buy to produce the goods and services you are selling. So if you sell computers, the cost of buying in the computers will be one such cost. In Blue Skies Travel's case, as they are in the travel business, the cost of airline tickets and hotel rooms are the raw material of their product, a holiday.

What we have left from our sales revenues after deducting the cost of sales, as these costs of 'making' are known, is the gross profit. This is really the only discretionary money coming into the business, over which we have some say on how it is spent. So the goal here is to keep these costs under tight control and aim for an improving gross margin percentage.

In the account shown in Table 4.1 you can see that Blue Skies have two sources of income, one from tours and one from insurance and other related services. They also, of course, have the costs associated with buying in holidays and insurance policies from suppliers.

The difference between the income of 1,416,071 and the cost of these 'goods' they have sold is just 160,948, which amounts to just

Table 4.1 Example of gross profit calculation for a service business

Blue Skies Travel profit and loss account for the year to 31 March

	£/$/€	
Income		
Tours sold	1,402,500	
Insurance and other services	13,571	
Total income	1,416,071	100%
Less cost of goods sold		
Tours bought	1,251,052	
Insurance and other services	4,071	
Total cost of goods sold	1,255,123	
Gross profit	160,948	11.37%

11.37 per cent of sales. That is the sum that the management have to run the business and not the much larger headline-making figure of nearly 1.5 million.

For a business that manufactures or assembles products from bought-in materials (see Table 4.2) the figures are a little more complex. In the first instance the basic sum is the same as for a service business. Take the cost of goods from the sales income and what's left is gross profit. However, in a business that makes things we will be holding raw materials and we only want to count into cost of goods sold the materials actually used. We do this by noting the stock at the start of the period, adding in any purchases made, and deducting the closing stock.

We also need to build in the labour cost in production and any overheads such as workshop usage, and deduct those in order to arrive at the gross profit.

Table 4.2 Example of gross profit calculation for a manufacturing business

	£/$/€	£/$/€	£/$/€	
Sales			100,000	100%
Manufacturing costs				
Raw materials opening stock	30,000			
Purchases in period	25,000			
	55,000			
Less Raw materials closing stock	15,500			
Cost of materials used		39,500		
Direct labour cost		18,000		
Manufacturing overhead cost				
Indirect labour	4,000			
Workshop heat, light and power	3,500			
Total manufacturing costs		7,500		
Cost of goods sold			65,000	
Gross profit			35,000	35%

J D Wetherspoon

Since opening their first pub, Marler's Bar, at Colney Hatch Lane in London in 1979, J D Wetherspoon's growth has been almost uninterrupted. Even in the summer of 2009 when pubs, according to the British Beer and Pub Association (BBPA), were shutting across the UK at a rate of 52 a week as landlords struggled in the economic gloom, Wetherspoon managed to open 33 new pubs, some in the exact same location as those that had failed. With sales of £950 million ($1,570 million) and profits of £64.8 million ($107 million), Tim Martin, the company's founder and chairman, claims that his business does best when the economy turns down. They focus on driving energy and labour costs down and so can maintain gross margins when all around are losing theirs. The company has an ongoing goal to reduce energy and water costs year on year in all of its 734 pubs. An example of their approach to driving down cost is the energy control system being introduced to reduce ventilation energy consumption in their kitchens.

Using temperature, smoke/steam and flow sensors, it detects the heat, steam and smoke created by cooking and reacts accordingly by altering the fan speed up and down when required. This reduces not only energy consumption but also heating and cooling losses, and saves money and time by reducing maintenance costs; and it also means that the equipment has a longer operating lifespan whilst needing fewer repairs.

Energy use before introducing the system was 52,464 kWh and 16,297 kWh afterwards. This saves 36,167 kWh per year, a 69 per cent reduction in their ventilation energy consumption, resulting in direct savings of £2,729 ($4,510) per pub. The payback on their investment is under two years.

Introduce profit (ie less cost) motivation

What gets measured gets done and what gets rewarded gets done again is certainly a message that resonates with most managers. But that still leaves the questions of what you want done and on what basis you should reward people. The first hint, in the business world, that there might be a more to motivation than rewards and redundancy came with Harvard Business School professor Elton Mayo's renowned Hawthorne studies. These were conducted between 1927 and 1932 at the Western Electric Hawthorne Works in Chicago. Starting out to see what effect illumination had on productivity, Mayo moved on to see how fatigue and monotony fitted into the equation by varying rest breaks, temperature, humidity and work hours, even providing a free meal at one point. Studying a team of six women workers, Mayo changed every parameter he could think of including increasing and decreasing working hours and rest breaks, until finally he returned to the original conditions. Every change resulted in an improvement in productivity, except when two 10-minute pauses morning and afternoon were expanded to six five-minute pauses. The women felt that these frequent pauses upset their work rhythm.

Mayo's conclusion was that showing that 'someone upstairs cares', engendering a sense of ownership and responsibility, were important motivators that could be harnessed by management and that money didn't matter anywhere near as much as managers believed it did.

Link rewards to margins

Ultimately the CCCO wants lower costs to play an important role in profit creation, rather than relying solely on higher sales, which in any event may be hard, if not impossible, to achieve at every stage in the economic cycle. It follows that any financial incentive should be linked to the gross profit achieved rather than to, say, sales or the volume of production, either of which could be achieved at disproportionate cost.

The dangers of rewarding sales

Often the first non-salary incentive on offer in a business is sales commission, the attraction lying in the fact that it is apparently cost neutral. The theory is that as rewards are paid out of additional revenue, they don't actually cost the business anything. The problem here is that the organization can become so fixated in its quest for the next deal that costs (and the risk of future costs) go out of the window. The toxic asset mountains acquired by banks in their headlong rush for growth is a prime example. On a smaller scale, a London-based lighting company, Atrium, saw its profits more than double after changing to rewards based on gross profit rather than sales. Instead of being weak on price, the sales team, seeing that they would be giving away their own money if they yielded in negotiations, stood firm. They tightened up on all the extraneous costs associated with selling such as credit limits, the length of time consignment stock could be held, and ensured efficient delivery, going for a single drop rather than the more relaxed 'anything to please the client'.

Avoiding the overtime trap

Overtime, that is, any work over the basic working hours included in an employment contract, usually can't be imposed as regulations such as those in Europe say that most workers can't be made to work more than an average of 48 hours a week. Employees can, however, agree to work longer. There is no requirement to pay a premium for overtime work but in practice this almost invariably occurs.

Research projects on overtime working conducted by Cranfield School of Management and Cambridge University shine a light on the scale of this area of activity. A premium of time and a half applies to most overtime workers in the United States, whilst double time, time and a quarter, and time and a third are other common multiples found elsewhere. The average weekly overtime in all industries in Japan, the United States and the UK is roughly between three and four hours. In the UK alone, paid overtime was equivalent to around 1.5 million full-time jobs.

So overtime on premium pay is a big extra cost to business that should result in extra output. In theory firms should get more output for the extra cost, but researchers generally conclude that overtime is associated with poor management, poor planning and poor controls. In fact, in most cases average costs per unit of output rise more than the value of any extra revenue generated, and more often than not the costs themselves are the only elements to increase.

The reason is clear. Employees working average overtime hours in most countries would receive in excess of 20 per cent of total direct remuneration in the form of overtime pay. That's too big a sum for them to just sit back and wait for, so they have to manufacture circumstances for overtime to seem necessary. Overtime is often easier to get approval for than adding headcount, and can be approved by first-line supervisors. So overtime creep occurs and it gradually becomes accepted custom and practice.

Approval for overtime should be kept as a prerogative of senior management, and used sparingly, if at all. Those managers supervising overtime should be required to do so within their normal pay scale. That alone usually stops the practice dead.

Motivate without money

Frederick Hertzberg, professor of psychology at Case Western Reserve University in Cleveland, discovered that distinctly separate factors were the cause of job satisfaction and job dissatisfaction. His research revealed that five factors – achievement, recognition, responsibility, advancement and the attractiveness of the work itself – stood out as strong determinants of job satisfaction, working as cashless motivators. Weighing against these were a similar number of reasons for dissatisfaction: organizational policy, supervision, administration, working conditions and salary. Hertzberg called these causes of dissatisfaction 'hygiene factors'. He reasoned that the lack of hygiene will cause disease, but the presence of hygienic conditions will not, of itself, produce good health. So the lack of adequate 'job hygiene' will cause dissatisfaction but hygienic conditions alone will not bring about job satisfaction; to do that you have to work on the determinants of job satisfaction.

All this suggests that the diligent CCCO should be on the lookout for ways to motivate staff but without incurring cost. This should not be too difficult as money only featured directly in 1 of the 10 factors that govern motivation. Look out for opportunities to praise, to give staff additional responsibilities, and for ways to make work more interesting. 3M, Hewlett Packard and Google, for example, encourage employees to bootstrap company time and use that to pursue individual projects. The Post-it note was born out of this strategy to make work more interesting, rather than by piling costs into the R&D department.

Review your products and services

Selling the wrong products to the wrong people at the wrong price is a sure-fire way to rack up costs with little prospect of getting a worthwhile return. Just because you are making a product or service and your customers are happy and coming back for more doesn't mean you should continue doing so. Sometimes, as the Unilever case study shows, doing less now is the best way to end up with a better business in the future.

Unilever

In the spring of 2009 nearly every bank in the world was selling off any product group that was not core and even a few that were. The Royal Bank of Scotland put a fifth of its assets into a separate business ready to be sold off, leaving the management free to concentrate on the part that might possibly have a future. A decade earlier, in September 1999 to be precise, Unilever, a €34 billion (£30 billion, $50 billion) business employing some 300,000 people in 90 countries and the name behind such brands as Magnum, Omo, Dove, Knorr, Ben & Jerry's, Lipton, Slim-Fast, Iglo, Unox and Becel, announced its intention to focus on fewer, stronger brands in order to 'promote faster growth and improved margins'. Over the following four years Unilever set out to whittle its brands down to just 400 from the 1,600 it started out with. At the same time it shook up its top management, splitting the company into two separate global units: food, and home and personal care.

You don't have to take quite as long as Unilever did to remove products from your portfolio. Budget airline Ryanair took just a few days to cut back its winter flight schedule when faced with the cost rise imposed by the UK government's departure tax. They stripped 16 aircraft from Stansted routes, reducing their capacity by 40 per cent, switching to other less costly European bases. They took this decision four months before the new tax was due to come into effect.

Costing to eliminate unprofitable products and services

Not all of a business's products will always be profitable. Settling down to allocate 'real' fixed costs to products can be something of an eye opener to managers. Look at the example in Table 4.3. The business manufactures three products. Product C is bulky, complicated and a comparatively slow seller. It uses all the same sorts of equipment, storage space and sales effort as products A and B, only more so. When fixed costs are allocated across the range, it draws the greatest share.

Table 4.3 Product profitability 1

	A	B	C	Total
	£	£	£	£
Sales	30,000	50,000	20,000	100,000
Variable costs	20,000	30,000	10,000	60,000
Allocated fixed costs	4,500	9,000	11,500	25,000
Total costs	24,500	39,000	21,500	85,000
Operating profit	5,500	11,000	(1,500)	15,000

This proves something of a shock. Product C is losing money, so it has to be eliminated, which will produce the situation shown in Table 4.4.

Fixed costs will not change, so the 25,000 has to be reallocated across the remaining two products. This will result in profits dropping from 15,000 to 5,000; therefore our conventional product costing system has given the wrong signals. We have lost all the 'contribution' that product C made to fixed costs, and any product that makes a contribution will increase overall profits. Because fixed costs cannot be ignored, it makes more sense to monitor contribution levels and to allocate costs in proportion to them.

Table 4.4 Product profitability 2

	A	B	Total
	£	£	£
Sales	30,000	50,000	80,000
Variable costs	20,000	30,000	50,000
New allocated fixed costs	8,333	16,667	25,000
Total costs	28,333	46,667	75,000
Operating profit	1,667	3,333	5,000

Looking back to Table 4.3, we can see that the products made the contributions shown in Table 4.5 (contribution = sales – variable costs).

Table 4.5 Allocating fixed costs by contribution level

		Contribution		Fixed cost allocated
		£	%	£
Product	A	10,000	25	6,250
	B	20,000	50	12,500
	C	10,000	25	6,250
Total		40,000	100	25,000

Now we can recast the product profit and loss account using this marginal costing basis, as shown in Table 4.6 (Table 7.5 in my book *Practical Financial Management*). Not only should we not eliminate product C, but because in contribution terms it is our most profitable product, we should probably try to sell more.

Strip out unnecessary product cost

Even where products and services are profitable, there are opportunities to strip out cost. One of the most productive areas to start

Table 4.6 Marginal costing product profit-and-loss account

	A	%	B	%	C	%	Total
	£	%	£	%	£	%	£
Sales	30,000		50,000		20,000		100,000
Marginal costs	20,000		30,000		10,000		60,000
Contribution	10,000	33	20,000	40	10,000	50	40,000
Fixed costs	6,250		12,500		6,250		25,000
Product profit	3,750	13	7,500	15	3,750	19	15,000

with is to establish exactly what customers really value and what they don't. IKEA, for example, decided early on that its core market segment (see later in this section for more on market segments) was happy to assemble many products themselves. Where other furniture stores sold tables, chairs and beds already built, IKEA sold them flat packed for self-assembly. That cut out several layers of cost: the product didn't have to be fully manufactured; it didn't occupy much store or warehouse space; and it didn't have to be delivered as customers would take the product home with them. This last feature, incidentally, is an extra benefit for IKEA's customers who don't want to wait the weeks and sometimes months that other suppliers take to get product delivered – and they don't want to have to wait in at home for deliveries either. IKEA passes part of these cost savings on to their customers in lower prices and puts the rest on its bottom line.

Don't rush into discounts

Discounts are in effect a cost to the business that gives them, and the higher the discount, the greater the greater the effective cost. Price is the easiest and fastest element of the marketing mix to change and as such there is a great temptation to drop prices when the pressure is on. There are a number of important considerations when it comes to considering dropping prices:

- Price and quality are closely associated, so if you drop your prices faster and further than competitors do, customers may suspect that standards are dropping. There is, after all, a strong belief that your only get what you pay for.
- You have to sell an awful lot more of a discounted product to make the same amount of profit. Look at Table 4.7. This shows that in order to make the same amount of gross profit, a business discounting by 20 per cent would have to sell 67 per cent more product. The logic is simple. Unless you can get your suppliers to share some of the pain and reduce their prices, your gross profit will drop by the amount of your discount.

The best strategy is to defend your selling price by emphasizing the value of your proposition compared with those of your competitors. If necessary, add in some non-price elements such as 1 free for every 10 ordered. Where you absolutely have to give way on price, do so selectively and only where you can trade that discount for an equally valuable concession from a customer. This could include faster payment terms, increased volumes and an exclusive supply agreement or long-term contract.

Table 4.7 The true cost of discounting

Selling price £/$/€	Volume sold	Gross profit per unit sold £/$/€	Total gross profit £/$/€
100	100	50	5,000
80	100	30	3,000
80	167	30	5,010

Sell to the right market segment

Whilst the customer is always right, that doesn't mean they are always right for you. Most businesses end up doing too much for too many different types of business. The surest way to get costs down is to focus on the customers that work best for you. Ryanair know that their core customers want low prices and are prepared to forgo the frills, whilst British Airways believes their customers want a cooked English breakfast and a free newspaper. They can both be right, but usually that means setting out your stall to serve specific targeted customer groups, rather than trying to please everyone. The ultimate aim is to identify a market segment that gives you a unique edge and the opportunity to keep prices up whilst driving costs down.

Judy Lever and Vivienne Pringle started Blooming Marvellous back in 1983. The triggers for their starting up in business were wanting to start families and a love of fashion clothing. That left them with a wide market to aim at, from party and wedding dresses to blouses, shirts, ties, skirts and business suits. After experimenting with a range of ideas, it was only when they narrowed down their focus to a specific market segment, fashion-conscious mothers-to-be, that they realized they had found a market big enough to be worth their attention and with few competitors to put undue pressure on sale prices. The other big advantages to focusing on just one segment were that they had fewer suppliers to deal with and so could negotiate better prices, and their production processes were greatly simplified and their route to market was easier to target. Their costs fell off dramatically following their new strategy.

Initially they outsourced work to a small factory, some fabric suppliers, and eventually to a small distribution centre. After a year or so of modest sales they felt confident enough to set up their first business premise, a 1,200 square foot warehouse on a business park, staffed by four of the women who had been working in their distribution centre.

The company now employs 150 people, has 14 shops and has extended its range to include nursery products, toys, themed bedroom accessories and a separate brand called Mini Marvellous that caters for children aged two to eight years. Over a third of sales come directly via their website (www.bloomingmarvellous.co.uk).

Materials and their usage

The raw materials used to make up the product or service sold by a business can take up anything from 20 to 40 per cent of sales. With the possible exception of employment costs, it will be the biggest cost area and so fertile ground for pruning. Everything from finding suppliers who need your business more than your existing ones do, to cutting back waste and eliminating theft can add valuable percentage points to your gross margin.

Review suppliers

Finding suppliers is not too difficult; finding good ones that need you more than you need them is less easy. Business-to-business directories such as Kelly Search (www.kellysearch.co.uk), Kompass (www.kompass.co.uk) and Applegate (www.applegate.co.uk) between them have global databases of over 2.4 million industrial and commercial companies in 190 countries, listing over 230,000 product categories. You can search by category, country and brand name.

There is no point in changing to a new supplier only to find that whilst their headline cost is lower, they are making that lost ground up in other and perhaps more costly ways. You should check the supplier's:

- terms of trade;
- level of service;
- who else they supply (so that you can get feedback from their customers);
- what guarantees and warranties are on offer;
- price (make sure they are competitive);
- Finally, that you will enjoy doing business with them.

Don't leave any area out when looking for lower material costs. As well as suppliers of goods, service providers including insurance companies, utilities and banks are all well used to being negotiated with, as are accountants and lawyers.

Use fewer suppliers, ones who need your business

Dividing your business between too many suppliers is usually costly and inefficient. Only rarely does it make sense to have more than two or three suppliers. One should get the bulk of your business, and so you should ensure you achieve good volume discounts. One should supply smaller volumes but be reminded of the potential to replace your main supplier if the latter gets out of line. The third should be approved in that you have actually tried them out and regularly invite them to quote for your business or at least keep their prices under review.

Obviously you can't follow this strategy for every bought-in supply but you can for those that are important to you and to the supplier (see Figure 4.1).

	Value to you	
	Low	High
Low	You don't matter much to each other, so keep abreast of lowest prices	Supplier has the balance of power – look for alternative suppliers
High	You have the balance of power – don't overplay your hand	Potential for win-win outcomes that should be good for price negotiations

(Left axis label: Value to supplier)

Figure 4.1 The supplier–buyer balance of power

Find lower-cost substitute materials

Ultimately if you are in a weak negotiating position for vital supplies that make up an important part of your cost structure, you will have to consider using alternative lower-cost materials that can ideally be used in a more efficient manner. This could also be an opportunity to burnish your green credentials, as the John Roberts case study illustrates.

John Roberts Company: doing well by doing good

The John Roberts Company, based in Minneapolis, Minnesota, a commercial printer founded in 1951 by Robert Keene and John Chelberg, produces annual reports, brochures, catalogues, forms, direct mail and limited-edition fine-art prints. They use leased towels as wipers for press clean-up, sending them to an industrial laundry for cleaning and leaving it to deal with the problem of disposing of surplus ink and spent solvents. The company used a single highly volatile cleaning solvent, which, while working well for John Roberts, was a disaster for the laundry.

The local regulatory agency that oversees the sanitary sewer system warned the laundry that the level of solvent being washed out of the towels caused their effluent vapours to exceed the lower explosive limit. The challenge was for John Roberts and the industrial laundry to come up with a substitute cleaning agent that eliminated the danger, added no extra costs to either party and ideally saved money.

John Roberts worked with their trade association, the Printing Industry of Minnesota, Inc. (PIM), and set about working out a solution. First they examined the nature of the solvents used to clean the presses, to see if a cheaper, less volatile substitute could be used. During the audit of the process John Roberts discovered that the solvent they were using was so powerful that half simply evaporated before the work could be performed – a total waste of materials. They changed to a more appropriate and less toxic solvent and by using this more prudently achieved a saving of more than $18,000 (£11,000) in the first year. Whilst searching out substitutes they discovered a better way to operate their clean-up process. Before wipers are sent to the laundry, they are spun in a centrifuge bought for

$15,000 (£9,000), which extracts spent solvent that is now reused throughout the plant, saving the company more than $34,000 (£20,500) a year. This positive experience contributed to John Roberts's proactive review of their impact on the environment. Through their long-term efforts to recycle materials that would otherwise have ended up in a landfill, John Roberts have enabled their operations to achieve carbon-neutral status.

Buy in bulk or online

Consider buying in bulk or on longer-term contracts, but only if the discount is higher than your cost of capital. Look back to Chapter 3 to see how to work out if a discount is worth having. Joining an online buying group such as Buying Groups (www.buyinggroups.co.uk), Power Purchasing Group (www.ppg.co.uk) and e-Three (www.e-three.com) helps buyers to join forces and, by buying in bulk, usually getting better prices and terms of trade.

Whitbread goes in for e-sourcing

With commodity prices rising significantly, the pressure on margins for the hospitality industry is immense, so companies are looking to technology to mitigate such substantial cost increases. In December 2008, UK food and beverage firm Whitbread announced a saving of 16 per cent in a central area of procurement: chips, potato wedges and mashed potato. The company, which serves over 110,000 customers in some 500 venues each week, claims that the successful use of e-auctions will save it around £400,000 ($660,000) per year.

Sourcing supplies using traditional negotiating methods can take a week or more, but by using an e-auction Whitbread was able to take in 60 bids from four vendors and complete the entire buying process in under an hour. Whitbread's auction was run by eThree, using Oracle Sourcing technology, with prospective suppliers requiring less than an hour of training. Participating suppliers could see quickly if their bid slipped in the ranking and so submit a lower bid. Whitbread set the bidding parameters, then stepped aside, leaving prospective vendors to submit bids that were then ranked.

Negotiate better prices

Fewer than 1 in 20 owner-managers negotiate for better deals from their suppliers, and managers, with the exception of professional buyers, are not much more likely to either. This, however, is one area where it should be possible to strip a percent or two out of costs and add them to the bottom line as the result of just a few minutes' work.

Negotiating is as much a science as an art. There are a few immutable rules; easily understood but invariably difficult to execute:

- Aim high at the outset. Unless you can find the point of resistance, you can't find the outer limits of your negotiating range.
- You must be prepared to walk away from a deal and make that evident if you are to have any negotiating leverage. To achieve this you must have prepared plans B and C ready to execute if the terms you want can't be achieved. For example, have other suppliers in the frame too; or have plans to buy substitute materials and do without them altogether.
- Search out a range of variables to negotiate other than price that might be of value to the seller. Delivery date, payment terms, quantities, currencies, shared future profits and know-how swaps are just a handful of areas rich in negotiating possibilities.
- Never give a concession away: anything given for nothing is seen as being worth nothing. Instead, trade concessions and always put the highest value possible on the concession. 'We will pay 30 per cent upfront rather than the 20 per cent you're asking for (a gain for the seller) if you bring the price down

to £1.2 million rather than the £1.3 million you're asking' (a gain for the buyer) is the place to start if you hope to hit a £1.25 million final price.

- Talk as little as possible. The less you say, the less you can give away.
- Once you have put a proposition on the table, shut up. The first to blink is the loser.

Companies such as Collective Purchasing (www.collectivepurchasing.co.uk) collect pricing information to help you negotiate without compromising on quality.

Booths

Booths, a chain of classy supermarkets covering the North of England counties of Cheshire, Cumbria, Lancashire and Yorkshire, with some 26 outlets, holds a market position somewhere between Marks & Spencer and Waitrose. Entering one of their stores you could be forgiven for thinking you were in an upmarket branch of Sainsbury's in the Home Counties. Nothing too unique about that, but scratch a bit deeper and what makes Booths different stands out a mile. First, they are independent and in family ownership. Edwin Booth, chairman since 1997, represents the sixth generation of Booths to run the business since it was founded in Blackpool in 1847. The company's turnover and profit in 2009 were £253 million ($418 million) and £10 million ($16.5 million) respectively, which neatly puts paid to the old family business saw of 'from clogs to clogs in three generations'.

The family still owns 96 per cent of the shares, with the balance being owned by the staff. Aside from ownership and heritage, the company is distinctive in steering clear of trying to get so big as to be impersonal. They have only acquired two businesses in their 162-year history. Booths have found a way to get muscle in other ways. In October 2008 they formed a trading alliance with Waitrose, using that to bargain down prices with suppliers. Eventually they hope to actually combine their orders and so increase purchase volumes, which in turn should allow them to negotiate even keener discounts.

Strip out waste

The challenge here is to strip out waste or find ways to step up yield. If you are working on your own this will probably not be a fertile field, but once you have employees, however dedicated, the problems start. The classic question when people want to buy something is to ask them, 'If it were your money would you spend it this way?'

The food industry is perhaps the most visible industry with a waste problem. From farm to plate, some 20 million tonnes of food are wasted every year in the UK alone, with around a third of that the direct responsibility of businesses. But nearly every industry produces waste and that has cost implications for production efficiencies, disposal and a firm's capacity to meet an ever increasing array of environmental challenges and regulations.

Daily Bread

Working from the basement of a deli in Chelsea, Daily Bread was started in 1986 by making 35 delicious sandwiches and walking around local offices trying to sell them. The business is now part of the Hain Celestial Group, a leading natural and organic food and personal care products company. The group's other brands include Linda McCartney, and they have operations in North America and Europe. The company still makes delicious sandwiches and has earned a royal warrant to prove it, but more conventional routes to market have supplanted basket deliveries.

As with other companies that supply sandwiches to Marks & Spencer, Daily Bread is required to discard four slices from each loaf, the crusts and the first slice in. As well as being a sheer waste of food, the company was paying around £65,000 ($107,000) a year to send this food to be turned into gas for power generation.

As a result of advice from a UK government-sponsored body, Environwise, the company now sells its unwanted bread to a local farmer for use as animal feed. Benefits to the company include turning a cost into a revenue stream as they get £25 ($41) a tonne from the farmer. Also, the process emits no carbon dioxide and contributed to its green strategy, culminating in it being named the 10th greenest company in the UK, and THE greenest company in the food and drink sector in *The Sunday Times* Best Green Companies Awards 2009.

Eliminate theft and fraud

You may believe that just because your business sells no tangible products or is not a retailer with a regular influx of unknown and unknowable visitors that your risk from theft or fraud is low. You may feel even more secure if you don't handle cash or any form of face-to-face transaction. If you draw comfort from any of these positions, the chances are you are wrong. The statistics are truly scary.

A report by the US Small Business Administration (SBA) estimated in 2008 that employees rather than outsiders commit two-thirds of business thefts. The SBA also reported that nearly 10 per cent of businesses filing for bankruptcy cited a business calamity such as business theft or fraud as a cause of their financial difficulties. A survey commissioned by The Federation Against Software Theft has found that the items stolen by staff are not confined to the company's own products but range from computer software and digital downloads (film, music and video), which 10 per cent of staff admitted taking, through to printer paper and blank CDs (25 per cent) and pens and stationery (62 per cent). The FBI receives more than 300,000 reports of potential corporate theft every month and the Global Retail Theft Barometer, the world's largest and most comprehensive survey on the subject, reckons that retail shrinkage costs businesses worldwide in excess of £1 billion.

Perhaps the most alarming recent development is business identity theft, which, whilst serious and common, so embarrasses companies that they keep their victimization secret. One technique used here is to change the registered office address at Companies House and have goods delivered to the 'new' address. By the time suppliers realize what is happening the tricksters have moved on. Even the professionals in the field are at risk here. Namesafe, a business-identity protection firm, sued LifeLock, a competitor, according to papers filed in Tennessee in June 2008, claiming they had stolen its trademark and deceptively diverted traffic meant for Namesafe's website to LifeLock's own website. The suit claimed that LifeLock bought sponsored ads on major search engines and portals including Google, Yahoo, MSN and Hotbot, diverting users onto its site.

The Association of Certified Fraud Examiners (ACFE) estimates that the typical business will lose an average of 6 per cent of revenues from employee theft alone. Their tips for minimizing business theft are to trust no one, be extra careful in hiring and vigilant in supervision, implement basic controls across all areas of the organization, both internal and external, and never let one person control all aspects of a business area.

Cost-cutting assignment 4

Go back over this chapter and look for ways to cut the costs associated with making or assembling your product or service.

1 How does your gross profit margin compare with previous years and with the best in class in your sector?
2 Are all your products or services truly profitable, or should you ditch some and concentrate more on others?
3 Do you have the best-value suppliers?
4 When did you last negotiate a discount and how successful were your negotiations?
5 Are there smarter, lower-cost ways to work?
6 What non-cash measures do you take now to motivate staff and are there others you could adopt?
7 What measures do you take to monitor and evaluate waste, theft and fraud?
8 Could you use substitute lower-cost materials in your production or assembly processes?

5
Trim overheads

- Applying cost-effective marketing strategies;
- Getting better value from internet operations;
- Travelling further for less;
- Trimming travel and subsistence budgets;
- Using utilities less.

As we saw in the preceding chapter, a business doesn't have access to all the cash that comes in from selling its products; it first has to buy in materials and services from outside. Those purchases are then crafted into a product or service and what is left after these costs have been incurred is the gross profit. The next raft of costs a business faces are the general operating costs of running the business – rent, rates, marketing, travel and so forth – that cannot be directly attributed to the volume of sales.

These costs are often called overheads, a term that has a derogatory connotation; and indeed, overheads are viewed by some as being optional. The feeling is that direct costs can be attributed directly to a product (see Chapter 1), whilst indirect costs cannot and so are fair game for the CCCO.

Table 5.1 sets out the typical items to be found in the operating expenses of a business. The figures are simply for illustration purposes and are not representative costs. An e-commerce business and a retail shop would have quite different levels of cost in each of these categories.

By running the percentages of cost alongside the absolute figures, the CCCO can get a quick feel for where costs might be getting out of line. For example, we can see in these figures that sales and marketing, travel and subsistence, telephone and internet,

Table 5.1 Profit and loss account showing typical operating cost items

	Last year		This year	
	£/$/€	%	£/$/€	%
Sales	1,000,000		1,200,000	
Less cost of sales	500,000		600,000	
Gross profit	500,000	50	600,000	50
Less operating costs:				
Sales and marketing	60,000	6	80,000	6.7
Travel and subsistence	30,000	3	40,000	3.3
Rent, rates, insurance	100,000	10	110,000	9
Utilities	20,000	2	25,000	2.1
Telephone and internet	60,000	6	80,000	6.7
Training	10,000	1	10,000	0.8
Admin and other salaries	160,000	16	200,000	16.7
Professional service and consultancy	5,000	0.5	5,000	0.4
Stationery and office supplies	5,000	0.5	6,000	0.5
Total operating cost	450,000		556,000	
Operating profit (gross profit – operating costs)	50,000	5	44,000	3.7

and admin and other salaries are all growing at a faster rate than the growth of the business. That in itself is not conclusive evidence that costs are out of line, but it would certainly point to a good place to start looking for savings.

Saving on sales and marketing

Sales and marketing are the area of cost that are most likely to have an impact on business performance. William Hesketh Lever, Unilever's founder, is credited with saying, 'Half the money I spend on advertising is wasted, and the trouble is I don't know which half.' (This quote, or one similar and with the same sentiment, is also attributed to John Nelson Wanamaker, a US retailer and one of the first to use large-scale advertising campaigns devised by advertising agencies.)

Advertising on a shoestring: how to get seen more for less

Tim Bell, now Lord Bell, formerly of Saatchi & Saatchi, has described advertising as 'essentially an expensive way for one person to talk to another'. It's certainly expensive. According to the Advertising Association, UK businesses spend £20 billion ($33 billion) a year on A&P (advertising and promotion), so if Lever's rule still applies, the CCCO has a £10 billion ($16.5 billion) cost-savings pot to tap into. The following questions should underpin all expenditure on A&P and in the answer to the last of them lies the key to achieving substantial cost savings:

■ What do you want to happen? Do you want prospective customers to visit your website, phone, write or e-mail you, return a card or send an order in the post?

■ Do you expect them to have an immediate need to which you want them to respond now, or is it that you want them to remember you at some future date when they have a need for whatever it is you are selling? The more you are able to identify a specific response in terms of orders, visits, phone calls or requests for literature, the better your promotional effort will be tailored to achieve your objective, and the more clearly you will be able to assess the effectiveness of your promotion and its cost versus its yield.

■ How much is that worth to you? Once you know what you want a particular promotional activity to achieve, it becomes a little easier to estimate its cost. Suppose a £1,000 ($1,652) advertisement is expected to generate 100 enquiries for your product. If experience tells you that on average 10 per cent of enquiries result in orders, and your profit margin is £200 ($330.40) per product, then you can expect an extra £2,000 ($3,304) profit. That 'benefit' is much greater than the £1,000 ($1,652) cost of the advertisement, so it seems a worthwhile investment.

Measuring results

This is the cost cutter's main tool when it comes to dealing with A&P expenditure. Judy Lever, co-founder of Blooming Marvellous, the upmarket maternity-wear company, believes strongly not only in evaluating the results of advertising, but in monitoring a particular medium's capacity to reach her customers. 'We start off with one-sixteenth-page ads in the specialist press,' says Judy. 'Then once the medium has proved itself we progress gradually to half a page, which experience shows to be our optimum size. On average there are 700,000 pregnancies a year, but the circulation of specialist magazines is only around the 300,000 mark. We have yet to discover a way of reaching all our potential customers at the right time – in other words, early on in their pregnancies.'

Choosing the media

The press – newspapers, magazines and journals – is the largest medium, attracting 40 per cent of all advertising expenditure. Then comes TV with 24 per cent, then the internet, accounting for nearly 16 per cent of expenditure, followed by direct mail (11.2 per cent), outdoors and transport (5.5 per cent), radio (2.8 per cent) and cinema (1.1 per cent). Of these, the fastest-growing segment by far is the internet, up by 40 per cent, followed by cinema (+10 per cent), whilst press and direct mail are shrinking.

The internet: the CCCO's best ally

The reason the internet is growing in popularity as an A&P resource lies in its proven cost effectiveness, the ease of measuring results and the speed with which messages can be changed in response to changing situations. Yield management, the process that maximizes usage and revenue, in the hotel and travel industries has become incalculably more efficient as a result of internet advertising.

The primary A&P spend for most businesses is on their website. (See later in this chapter for more on websites). There are also the millions of other websites and search engines that provide plenty of opportunities to get your message in front of your market. The main low-cost options are:

- Search engine advertising. For major search engines such as GoogleAdWords(www.google.com>BusinessSolutions>Earn revenue with AdWords), Yahoo Search Marketing (http://searchmarketing.yahoo.com) and Microsoft adCenter (https:adcenter.Microsoft.com), you will be invited to bid on the terms you want to appear for, by way of a set sum per click. Google, for example, offers a deal where you pay only when someone clicks on your ad, and you can set a daily budget stating how much you are prepared to spend, with $5 a day as the starting price.
- E-mail marketing is just like conventional direct mail sent by post, except with e-mail as the medium; to use it you buy e-mail databases relating to your target audience.
- Online display advertising, like advertising in newsprint, takes the form of words and images of varying sizes on websites that people looking for your product are likely to come across. The Audit Bureau of Circulations Electronic (www.abce.org.uk) audits website traffic.
- Viral marketing is the process of creating something so hot that recipients will pass it on to friends and colleagues, creating extra demand as it rolls out. Jokes, games, pictures, quizzes and surveys are examples.

■ Blogs are online spaces where the opinions and experiences of particular groups of people are shared. Online communities, MySpace for example, are an extension of this idea. Nielsen NetRatings reported in 2009 that over 2 billion community sites are viewed every month in the UK alone. Wikis – sites such as Wikipedia – are special types of blogs that allow users to contribute and edit content. These are spaces where you can make sure your product or service gets some visibility. Newsgator (www.newsgator.com) and Google Analytics (www.google.com/analytics) have blog indexing services to help you search out those appropriate to your business sector.

■ Podcasts, where internet users can download sound and video free, are now an important part of the e-advertising armoury.

Payment for most internet advertising uses a 'cost per' model, with the advertiser paying per view, click, visitor or – better still – an action such as placing an enquiry or registering on the site. The beauty of these payment terms is that unlike other media where you pay a set sum that is not dependent on the results you get, using these methods you only pay for what you get.

The Internet Advertising Bureau (www.iabuk.net) has a wealth of further information on internet advertising strategies as well as a directory of agencies that can help with some or all of these methods of promoting your business. Nielsen NetRatings (www.nielsen-netratings.com>Resources>FreeDataandRankings) provides some free data on internet advertising metrics.

Public relations: advertising for free

Most potential customers view all A&P activity with suspicion. Not unreasonably, they expect the seller to put a favourable a gloss on the 'facts' and may well stray rather far from the absolute truth on occasions.

Strangely enough, one medium the public are likely to trust is editorial information that appears in the press, online or on TV, and that is not paid for by the company concerned. Whilst journalists do a fair amount of ferreting out the truth, much of what they write is sent in by companies to get their message across – and putting information through the filter of an independent journalist seems to carry weight.

Chantal Coady, the Harrods-trained chocolatier who founded Rococo, was 22 when she wrote the business plan that secured her £25,000 ($41,300) start-up capital. The cornerstone of her strategy to reach an early break-even point lay in a carefully developed public relations campaign. By injecting fashion into chocolates and their packaging, she opened up the avenue to press coverage in such magazines as *Vogue*, *Harpers & Queen* and the colour supplements. She managed to get over £40,000 ($66,000) worth of column inches of space for the cost of a few postage stamps. This not only ensured a sound launch for her venture but eventually led to a contract from Jasper Conran to provide boxes of chocolates to coordinate with his spring collection.

With UK editors receiving an average of 80–90 press releases per week, make sure that you are making your latest newsworthy item public, but make sure it is free of puffery and jargon. PR Made Easy (www.prmadeeasy.com>Guides) provides 40 free guides on a range of PR topics as well as templates to help your write a press release.

Selling more for less

Selling is one of the most cost intensive areas of business. Salaries are high, as are expenses for travel, subsistence, communications and training. Recruitment costs are high too and salespeople tend to stay in one job for less time than most other workers. According to the US Bureau of Labor Statistics the median number of years that wage and salary workers had been with their current employer was 4.1 years in January 2009, little changed from 4.0 years in January 2006. So cost of recruitment also has to spread over a very short period.

There are two proven strategies for generating more sales for far less cost than recruiting more salespeople.

Retain more customers

Acquiring customers is an expensive process; they have to be found, wooed and won. Once you have them onside they cost less to keep, spend more money with you and are less price sensitive than new customers. Retaining them will do more than almost any other marketing strategy to grow your profit margin. According to research carried out by Bain (www.bain.com> ConsultingExpertise>Capabilities>CustomerStrategy&Marketing> Customer Loyalty) a 5 per cent increase in customer retention can improve profitability by 75 per cent. Here are the keys to retaining customers:

- Ninety-six per cent of complaints never get made; dissatisfied customers just go elsewhere. You need to find ways to listen to them – actively. Follow up phone calls, short questionnaires on reply-paid cards, blogs and mystery shopping are all successful listening strategies.
- Act on complaints. Ninety-four per cent of customers who complain will give their supplier another chance if they are dealt with quickly and fairly.
- Build loyalty by giving customers a reason to stay with you, such as discounts or VIP treatment, or by giving them something more than they expect, to show that you appreciate them and their business.

Outsource selling

If you are not going to be your business's main salesperson, you need to brace yourself for costs of around £80,000 ($132,000) a year to keep a good salesperson on the road, taking salary, commission and expenses into account. The problems with employing your own salespeople is that initially each one you take on won't sell enough to cover their costs and you may get the wrong person and so end up with just a big bill and no extra sales.

A less costly sales route is to outsource your selling to freelance salespeople. Here you have two options and both have the merit of shifting your costs from fixed to variable, always a desirable outcome for the CCCO:

- Employ a sales outsourcing company such as Selling People (www.sellingpeople.biz) or People per Hour (www. peopleperhour.com), who can find and manage a salesperson for you on a short-term basis.
- Find an agent for yourself, ideally one with existing contacts in your field who knows buyers personally and can get off to a flying start from day one. The Manufacturers' Agents' Association (www.themaa.co.uk>Finding an Agent) have a directory of commission agents selling in all fields of business. You pay £150 plus £26.25 VAT by credit card for an MAA Net Search allowing you to contact up to 20 agents in one search.

Internet: the universal cost cutter

No business, indeed no organization for that matter, can afford to ignore the internet. Over 1.5 billion people worldwide have an internet connection; 18 million households in the UK are online. Everything from books and DVDs, through computers, medicines, financial services, and on to vehicles and real estate is being sold or having a major part of the selling process transacted online. Holidays, airline tickets, software, training and even university degrees are bundled in with the mass of conventional retailers such as Tesco that fight for a share of the ever growing online market. The online gaming market alone has over 217 million users.

From the CCCO's perspective the power of the internet lies in global reach for virtual peanuts. Most major operational tasks can be performed for less. You can sell to a market in another continent for little more than the cost of a single airline ticket; tapping into a global recruitment market gives access to talent that might otherwise be impossible; having an online audience opens up other revenue opportunities. Once you have set up your shop front, got your shopping cart, arranged a payment system and organized fulfilment, all you have to do is 'stack the shelves'.

Low-cost selling online

The value of web transactions in the United States in 2008–09 was over $400 billion and in the UK alone was £55.5 billion, up from £19 billion in 2002; the value of sales to households as opposed to businesses over the same period doubled to £16 billion; £81 in every £100 spent in 2008–09 on the internet was used to buy physical goods. In the United States 16 million people visited jewellery websites, 35 million hit flower and gift sites and 42 million looked for travel-related products and services.

According to eMarketer (www.emarketer.com) 88 per cent of shoppers prefer online to conventional shopping because they can shop at any time; 66 per cent like being able to shop for more than one product and in many outlets at the same time; 54 per cent claim to be able to find products that are available only online; 53 per cent like not having to deal with salespeople; 44 per cent reckon product information is better online; and, perhaps the most revealing statistic of all, only 40 per cent preferred online to offline because they expected to find lower prices.

That last fact is good news for business as it indicates that there is scope for service to play an important part in a consumer's purchasing decision, and service is just what the internet can provide to complement a sale with an array of soft benefits at zero cost. Blogs, downloads, virtual tours, FAQs, 24/7/365 query answering, follow-up surveys and customer reviews all enhance the buying experience but once the systems are set up cost little to maintain.

Other internet cost reducers

You might be forgiven for thinking that a website is just for those selling on the internet; that, however, is just one of the many uses a website can be put to. These are some other areas in which the internet can help with cost reduction:

- Generating advertising revenue. Once you have a website you have 'readers' whom other people will pay to reach, just as they would if you had a hard-copy magazine. As this revenue comes without much cost attached, it is a margin-enhancing strategy, which in turn is the ultimate aim of cost cutting. You can sell space on your website yourself, but you should be too busy running your business to get diverted with this type of distraction. The easiest way to get advertising revenue is to get someone else to do the hard work. Google (www.google.com>Business Solutions>Earn revenue with AdSense), for example, matches advertisements to your site's content and you earn money every time someone clicks one. You can check out the dozens of other affiliate advertising schemes such as FastClick Ad Network, Click Bank and Revenue Pilot at Internet Ad Sales (www.internetadsales.com> Online Ad Networks)) a site that reviews all online advertising products and trends.
- Recruitment. You can advertise for staff on your own website. In that way you can be sure applicants will know something of your business and you could cut out most of the costs of recruitment, saving anything from a few hundred to several thousand pounds per appointment.
- Market research. By running surveys you can find out more about your customers' needs, check out if new products or services would appeal to them and monitor complaints and so prevent them becoming problems. You could even generate free knowledge about the market to support your PR, which in turn is free advertising.
- Save communication costs. Businesses get thousands of phone calls and letters asking essentially the same questions.

By having an FAQ (frequently asked questions) section on your website you can head off most of those and save time and money.

■ Add low-/no-cost extra value. By including information relating to your product, for example a weather chart or foreign-currency calculator if you are selling holidays, you will make your service better and different from those of competitors who don't have such features. You don't have to do the work yourself. Check out Bizezia (www.bizezia.com), RSS Feed Reader (http://rssfeedreader.com) and Yahoo (http://finance.yahoo.com/badges) to see the range of articles, calculators, tax calendars, online tutorials and financial information you can link, often for free, to your website.

Novacroft

Debra Charles's business, Novacroft, established in 1998 in Northampton with an inheritance from her parents, manages customer records for companies that issue pre-paid smart cards. Oyster cards are one of their major accounts and by 2009 Charles's company had a turnover of £6 million and was employing nearly 100 staff. The company's business model is based around using the internet to enable their customers to deliver a superior service at a lower cost. They manage online every aspect of smart-card functionality from the application form through record handling to loading information and credit onto those cards.

The company's web operations are also at the centre of their efforts to drive down their own costs. A recent study of the nature of queries they were handling led them to make improvements to their online information, which along with other steps to move service delivery online has led to savings in excess of £80,000 ($132,000) a year.

Saving on website design

Good website design is essential, with short loading time (use graphics, not photographs), legible text that is short and sweet, and an attractive layout. Research indicates that within three clicks, visitors must be captivated or they will leave. So clear signposting is necessary, including a menu on every page so that visitors can return to the homepage or move to other sections in just one click. But none of this has to cost a packet.

Doing it yourself

You probably already have a basic website writing tool with your Office software. If you use Microsoft, then at Microsoft Office Live (http://office.microsoft.com>Microsoft Office Live) you will find links to free web-design tools. You will also find literally hundreds of packages from £50 ($83) to around £500 ($825) that with varying amounts of support will help you create your own website. Web Wiz Guide (www.webwizguide.com>Know-ledgebase>Designing a Web Site) has a tutorial covering the basics of web page design and layout. BT Broadband office (www. btbroadbandoffice.com/businesstoday/0,9737,cats-5528530,00. html) is a direct link to dozens of articles on how to improve your website design. Top Ten Reviews (www.toptenreviews.com> Software>Website Creation) provides an annual report on the best website creation software rated by ease of use, help and sup-port, value for money and a score of other factors. The best buy when this book was being written was one-third of the price of the third-ranking programme.

Getting outside help

There are literally thousands of consultants who claim to be able to create a website for you. Prices start from £499 ($825), for which an off-the-peg website package will be tweaked slightly to meet your needs, to around £5,000 ($8,300), which will get you some-thing closer to tailor made. The Directory of Design Consultants (www.designdirectory.co.uk>Design Category>Internet) and Web Design Directory (www.web-design-directory-uk.co.uk) list hundreds of consultants, some one-man bands, others somewhat larger. You can look at their websites to see if you like what they do. Web Design Directory has some useful pointers on choosing a designer. If you are working within a set budget you could consider auctioning off your web-design project. With sites such a Get a Freelancer (www.getafreelancer.com) you state how much you are prepared to pay, with a description of the project, and freelancers around the world bid under your price, with the lowest bidder winning.

Thrifty visibility

There is not much point in building a website, however low the cost, if you get little traffic. Sure, some people will stumble across your site by accident, but it doesn't have to be like that. You could get high-cost SEO (search engine optimization) consultancy advice on how to get seen on the web. As 9 out of 10 visitors reach internet sites via a search engine or equivalent, you certainly need to aim for a position on the first few pages of any relevant search, be that products for sale or job vacancies to be filled. Type 'Indiba' into Google's search pane and you will draw a blank. Put in 'fish restaurants Truro' in and at the top of page one will pop: 'Indiba, one of the finest fish and seafood restaurants in Cornwall'. The restaurant really is great, but the owners have filled their website with words and phrases that an online searcher might use in their quest.

Here are some frugal steps you can take to get the right people to look at your website messages.

Self-optimize your website

If you want to be sure of getting listed appropriately in a search engine, first make a list of the words that you think a searcher is most likely to use when looking for your products or services. For example, a repair garage in Penzance could include keywords such as car, repair, cheap, quick, reliable, insurance, crash and Penzance in the home page to pull in searchers looking for a competitive price and a quick repair. As a rule of thumb, for every

300 words you need a key word or phrase to appear between 10 and 15 times. Search engines thrive on content, so the more relevant the content the better. You can use products such as that provided by Good Keyword (www.goodkeyword.com), who have a free Windows software programme to help you find words and phrases relevant to your business and provides statistics on how frequently those are used. Keywords Gold is their paid-for product, priced at $49 (£30) and which has several additional filters and tools to help you refine your keyword lists.

Search engine algorithms also like important, authoritative and prestigious terms. So whilst you may not be able to boast 'by Royal Appointment', if you can get your press releases quoted in the *Financial Times*, your comments included in postings on popular blogs or your membership of professional institutes and associations into your home page, your chances of being 'spidered' will rise accordingly.

Get and give free links

Next on the list of strategies is to get your website linked to other sites with related but not competing information. So if you are selling garden pots, websites that sell plants, gardening tools, fencing or compost are likely to have people hitting their sites who would be of value to you. Being linked to dozens of other sites improves your chances of being spotted by a search engine. You can offer the sites in question a link to your site as a quid pro quo and you could both benefit from the relationship.

Keep submitting your URL

Don't forget to submit the URL (Uniform Resource Locator) of your website domain name to search engines and reregister on a regular basis. Check on the search engine websites for the section headed 'Submit your site'. For example, for Yahoo this is http://search.yahoo.com/info/submit.html; registering is free. Most search engines offer a premium registration service that involves a fee of some sort but does guarantee a better degree of exposure.

Yahoo Directory Submit (www.yahoo.com/dir/submit/intro) costs $299 (£183) a year and claims to put you ahead of the herd, and their sponsored search service paid for by the 'click' aims to get you even more visibility.

Submitting to each search engine repeatedly is time consuming so, as you might expect, the process can be automated using URL submission software such as that provided by WebPosition (www.webposition.com) or Web CEO (www.webceo.com) for between $150 (£90) and $400 (£240). These programs will not only ensure that your entry in search engines is kept up to date, but will provide tips on improvement and tools to report on your search-engine ranking.

Use a submission service

Whilst you can build words into your website that will help search engines find you, there are also professionals whose job it is to move you up the rankings. Submission services such as those provided by Submit Express (www.submitexpress.xo.uk), Rank4u (www.rank4u.co.uk) and Wordtracker (www.wordtracker.com) have optimization processes that aim to move you into the all-important top-10 ranking in key search engines. Payment methods vary; for example, Rank4u have a no placement, no fee deal where they only get paid once they have achieved the positioning you want. 123 Ranking (www.123ranking.co.uk) have optimization packages aimed at small and new businesses for from £199 ($330) per annum. Search Engine Guide (www.searchengineguide.com>Search Engine Marketing) have a guide to all aspects of search-engine marketing.

Paid inclusion and placement

If you don't want to wait for search engines to find your website and want to avoid the expense of costly SEO consultancy advice, you can pay to have your web pages included in a search-engine directory. That won't guarantee you a position, so for example if your page comes up at 9,870 in Google's list then the chance of a customer slogging their way to your page is zero. The only way to be sure you appear early in the first page or two of a search is to advertise in a paid placement listing. For major search engines such as Google AdWords (www.google.com>Business Solutions> Earn revenue with AdWords), Yahoo Search Marketing (http:// searchmarketing.yahoo.com) and Microsoft adCenter (https: adcenter.Microsoft.com), you will be invited to bid on the terms you want to appear for, by way of a set sum per click.

The best of the rest: motoring and travel expenses

Running down the remaining operating expenses provides a rich harvest of cost-cutting opportunities. Obviously, if you run a fleet of hundreds of delivery vehicles and have sales and support staff shooting all over the world, this will be a priority cost area. But even the smallest business can realize big cost reductions. Here are the main areas that to a greater or lesser extent affect most organizations.

Vehicle costs

The Institute of Car Fleet Management (ICFM) reckons that the difference in cost between a well-run fleet of vehicles and one that has no effective control and management is 25 per cent. Simple cost reduction options in this area include:

- Get greener vehicles. Low-emission vehicles cost less to tax and insure, are fuel efficient and attract fast tax write-down rates, in some cases as much as 100 per cent of the purchase price in the first year.
- Use a fleet fuel card. These can be obtained from the main oil companies such as BP, Shell, Esso and Texaco. Cost benefits of card use include a discount on fuel, a single national price, free information on vehicle mileage and other vehicle management matters, prevention of fraudulent claims, and no

working capital tied up in fuel tanks. The Fuel Card People (http://www.thefuelcardpeople.co.uk/compare/compare2.php) have a comparison website to help find the best card for your needs.

■ Change to LPG fuel. LPG typically reduces running costs by up to 40 per cent through lower-taxed fuel, lower maintenance and longer engine life. Though there is a conversion cost, this can often be spread across fuel usage on a contact basis. The Flogas website (www.flogas.co.uk/autogas/savings) has a calculator to show annual savings dependent on vehicle and annual mileage.

■ Train your drivers. Teach your drivers basic efficient-driving techniques: have the right tyre pressures, accelerate slowly, half fill the fuel tank and plan the travel route carefully. These alone can cut costs by up to 10 per cent.

Travel on a budget

Once employees get an expense account, they often lose all sense of perspective. They see the rack rate for staying in a good four-star hotel is £200 ($330) and think that's what they should pay. With just a modicum of effort it is possible to stay in a similar-grade hotel for between half and one-third of that price. Ways to cut costs here include:

■ Set a cost budget. Give staff who travel to sell or support customers a specific expense budget and let them figure out the best hotel and travel deals. Armed with details of websites such as Skyscanner (www.skyscanner.net) and Late Rooms (www.laterooms.com), that both let you search for the lowest-cost option on the days surrounding a preferred travel date, it should be possible to make significant cost savings.

■ Use a travel service. American Express, for example, operate a business-travel programme that claims to be 7 to 11 per cent lower than online travel agencies when comparing total trip costs, including air, hotel and car rental. In addition, management information reports are provided, detailing travel patterns alongside suggestions for further cost savings. They even incorporate CO2 emissions data to track a firm's travel carbon footprint.

■ Make some trips virtual. Low- or no-cost video conferencing can be used for some client and in-house team meetings.

Utilities and telecommunications

Every business needs heat, light, water, power and communications systems. The question really is whether these have to cost so much. 1E, a software solutions provider, calculated in 2009 that it would be possible to save over $2.8 billion (£1.69 billion) in the United States just by turning off business PCs. In the UK and Germany £300 million ($500 million, €340 million) and £800 million ($1,300 million, €918 million) could be saved in this way. 1E estimated that if the world's 1 billion PCs were powered down for just one night, this would save enough energy to light up New York City's Empire State Building – inside and out – for over 30 years.

So the conclusions are:

■ Switch off. Encourage staff to switch off devices and lights when not in use. You can stimulate interest by measuring exactly how much power is used by individual devices – computers, printers, faxes, etc – or by user. It costs as little as £12 ($20) to get a unit to track the power used by a single plug. Around £29 ($48) a year can be saved just by turning off a single PC when not in use. Put shared equipment, faxes, water coolers, printers and vending machines on a seven-day timer. The payback period can be as little as a few weeks and thereafter there are significant cost savings to be had.

■ Turn down. According to the Carbon Trust, turning heating down by just one degree can cut those costs by upwards of 8 per cent. Keeping doors and windows closed when heating or air conditioning is on, and avoiding simultaneously heating and cooling at the same time, can increase such savings further. Bear in mind there are rules governing the required temperature of business premises.

- Lower lighting. Making use of natural lighting by selective positioning of work stations can reduce lighting costs by up to 19 per cent. Using individual lights rather than lighting an entire work area and using energy-saving light bulbs can help too.

- Phone free. Put all your staff and as many people as possible in other organizations that you regularly deal with on a VoIP (Voice over Internet Protocol) system. These use the internet as a connection route for making free or very low-cost telephone calls. Skype (www.skype.com) provides a free piece of software which, once installed, allows all users to speak free anywhere around the world. Aside from speech, text, landline and mobile phone calls, video conferencing and message answering services can be added for a modest cost. With a modest amount of discipline, phone bills could be cut by 50 per cent – more if you make a significant number of international calls. To find out what developments are in this field go to www.voipreview.org, www.voip-news.com and www.voip.org.uk.

Wages and salaries

Emergency cost cutting is dealt with in a later chapter and some ideas on eliminating overtime and motivating without money were covered in Chapter 4. Other ways to cut employment costs that can usually be achieved by natural wastage include:

- Eliminate unnecessary roles. For example, not all businesses need a receptionist full time, so job share the role with another task. For telephone cover use a company such as Office Response (www.office-response.co.uk; 0800 197 0286) or Office Answers (www.office-answers.co.uk; 0207 11 11 085), who offer a variety of services that amount to having a 'virtual receptionist'. Prices start from £17 ($28) a month with a £25 ($41) set-up cost. Office Answers offer a one-week free trial, after which if you are happy to proceed you commit to their minimum term of three months. The Royal Automobile Club in London's Pall Mall for years had a small post office on one side of its reception area and a kiosk selling papers, cigarettes and other small goods on the other. Neither operated all day and in 2009 they were combined, thus providing much longer opening hours, which both enhances guests' experience and increases sales, but with no additional costs.

- Get customers to work for you, for free. Gartner, a research firm, has findings to show that 60 per cent of customers prefer to carry out basic pre-purchase task such as checking stock availability of a product themselves, rather than relying on an employee. Blockbuster, a video-rental firm, plans to set up 3,000 kiosks in supermarkets and 24/7 locations, establishing a route to market that in effect makes the customer check themselves out.

- Training for free and nearly free. Training sounds like a cost increaser rather than a cost reducer, but that would be to misunderstand its value. Tom Frost, a former chairman of NatWest, reckoned that correcting mistakes accounted for between 25 and 40 per cent of the total cost of their service operations. Toyota Motors Europe (TME) have recently rolled out a centralized, computer-based training system for 80,000 staff at 28 independent sales and marketing companies in 48 countries, with the express goal of reducing costs. Check out: Business Balls (www.businessballs.com) for free business training, organization development, materials, exercises, videos, tools and templates; and Learn Direct (www.learndirect.co.uk/businessinfo), who provide e-learning, public and tailored training for business.

- Check you are paying the going rate for jobs and no more. The easiest way to find the going rate is to look at advertisements for similar jobs in your area or visit PayScale (www.payscale.com>for employers), where you can get accurate real-time information on pay scales.

Morgan Cars (www.morgan-motor.co.uk)

The Morgan Motor Company was formed in 1912 with the Reverend H G Morgan as chairman and his son as managing director. From the start it was very much a family business, with Morgan's sister Dorothy a regular entrant in reliability trials and gaining many first-class awards in a Morgan three-wheeler. The site of the first factory was on the Worcester Road leading into Great Malvern and the company has kept its operations in the county ever since. In 1991 business troubleshooter the late Sir John Harvey-Jones visited the company and offered some painful advice. The all-too-public nature of that advice, as it was shown on national television, was not easy to accept. Sir John, who had been invited in by Charles Morgan, an ITN cameraman and son of the then managing director Peter Morgan, was bewildered by the antiquated production processes leading to a three-year average delay between ordering and receiving a car.

Peter Morgan found much of the advice hard to accept as it called for a total overhaul of operating processes. The ensuring publicity had extended the order book even further so to some extent the pressure to change had evaporated. Charles, meantime, kept in periodic contact with Sir John, and when he took over the company began to adopt many of his earlier recommendations. Sir John's initial appraisal led Charles to spend three years completing a part time MBA in manufacturing management at Coventry University. Then he began to employ qualified engineers who overhauled design and production processes, standardizing materials across the product range. The company produced the Aero 8 – the first completely new Morgan for 30 years. The car is Europe's first AIV (aluminium-intensive vehicle) and has perhaps the best power-to-weight ratio of any current production car.

Today the company turns over £26 million, produces 700 cars a year, nearly double the number produced in 1991 when Sir John visited. More important, the profit margin has risen fivefold from between 2 and 3 per cent to around 12 per cent. According to Charles Morgan, the future of the company depends on the development and training of the workforce.

Go paperless

The paperless office, the vision of the 1980s, was one of the great values to be derived from computers and the rapid fall in the cost of hard-drive storage. It hasn't happened and may never do so. Paper is adaptable, compliant, useful for casual ad-hoc reading, and valuable as a work-in-progress medium for drafts and the like. It has proved itself a great survivor. Far from cutting back on paper, business use is growing. According to the US Environmental Protection Agency, the average office worker in the United States uses 10,000 sheets of copy paper each year, equivalent to 4 million tons nationally.

Whilst going paperless remains a pipe dream, even the smallest business could make substantial savings with some modest changes in work practices. The cost savings don't just come from reduced usage, but also from trimming storage space and postage; time spent addressing and filling envelopes is eliminated and using e-invoicing can speed up cash flow. Any firm sending out a few hundred letters and invoices a month could save upwards of £2,000 ($3,300) annually in this area. Research by document management company Macro 4 claims the cost of wasted printing – pages you didn't mean to print or decide not to use – amounts to £400 million ($660 million) per year for the average FTSE company, and only 58 per cent of IT directors monitor or manage office printing costs. Assuming a degree of exaggeration, there are still substantial savings to be made in office stationery. These are some examples of recent paper-saving initiatives:

- DHL, the distribution company, rolled out e-invoicing across Europe and by 2008 had cut out 336,000 paper invoices a year in the UK alone, saving 15 per cent of the paper, printing and postage costs associated with traditional billing.
- London law firm S J Berwin saved £700,000 ($115,600) in storage costs by going to electronic document management.
- The Scottish Executive, the devolved government of Scotland, installed an EDM (electronic document management) system in 2005, so making annual savings of over £500,000

($826,000) in space costs, time spent filing and searching for information.

- Richard Keyt, a solo business attorney in Arizona established in 1980, went 100 per cent paperless in 2005. Since then he has added over 350 new paying clients and taken on three attorneys and four legal assistants.

The California Integrated Waste Management Board (www. ciwmb.ca.gov/BizWaste/OfficePaper/QuickTip.htm) provides several pages of useful tips on cutting business paper. Four of their quick wins are:

- Accept minor handwritten corrections.
- Set computer defaults to double-sided.
- Route memos and newsletters around offices instead of making a copy for each person.
- Promote a 'Think before you copy' attitude.

Cost-cutting assignment 5

Go back over this chapter and look for ways to cut the overhead costs associated with operating your business.

1 How does your operating profit margin compare with previous years and with the best in class in your sector?
2 Are there steps you can take to reduce your wages bill?
3 Do you have to use so much paper and office supplies?
4 When did you last review your travel and subsistence costs?
5 Are you using the internet to best advantage in driving down operating costs?
6 What measures do you take to monitor utility costs?
7 Could you use more cost-effective marketing and promotional strategies?

6
Minimize finance and tax costs

- Finding free money;
- Cutting the cost of bank finance;
- Reducing the tax take;
- Easing back on auditing costs.

After operating profit the remaining three big cost areas are: financing costs, that is, interest payments and any expenses associated with raising money; accountancy and audit fees; and tax. Such costs can easily consume up to half any profits from operations and as such need to be kept firmly in the CCCO's sights. The reason for separating these costs from the run-of-the-mill overheads lies in accountability. Line managers in any business have little say in how these costs are arrived at. The government of the day sets the interest rate (up to a point, as even they are in the hands of the global economic climate) and the corporation and sales/VAT tax rates. True line managers can influence how much money is required to run the business by such factors as better control of working capital. But at the end of the day all costs that eat into the operating profit are mostly in the hands of the board and external economic events.

That doesn't mean the CCCO can't cut these costs; it just means that they will have to do most of the cutting themselves and can expect little help from others in the business. Typically, such non-operating costs, as they are generically known, can destroy half of the operating profits, so there is much to go for.

Interest and finance costs

Raising money usually entails incurring an arrangement fee, an ongoing cost for having use of the cash – interest in the case of a lender or dividends for an investor – and providing a viable exit route so the cash can be returned. There are plenty of different ways to finance a business and a myriad of costs that can be negotiated down or even away altogether.

Free money

Strangely enough, there is such a thing as a free lunch in the money world. It comes in the form of either a benevolent government whose agenda is either to get businesses to locate in an area more full of sheep than customers, or to pioneer new technologies. In addition, businesses, newspapers and magazines run competitions galore offering prizes to the best-run, fastest-growing or biggest exporting business and so forth. For the sponsor the reward is publicity and good stories and for the business founders there is money, perhaps as much as £50,000 ($79,419).

Gaining grants

Government agencies at both national and local-government level as well as some extra-governmental bodies such as the EU offer grants, effectively free or nearly free money in return for certain behaviour. It may be to encourage research into a particular field, stimulate innovation or employment or to persuade a company to locate in a particular area. Grants are constantly being introduced (and withdrawn), but there is no system that lets you know automatically. You have to keep yourself informed. Business Link (www.businesslink.gov.uk>Finance and grants>Grants and government support), has advice on how to apply for a grant as well as a directory of grants on offer. Microsoft Small Business Centre (www.microsoft.com/uk/businesscentral/euga/home.aspx)

has a European Union Grant Advisor with a search facility to help you find which of the 6,000 grants on offer might suit your business needs. Grants.Gov (www.grants.gov) is a guide to how to apply over 1,000 federal government grants in the United States.

Winning competitions

There are thousands of annual awards around the world aimed at new or small businesses. Most are based around a business plan or other presentation of your business ideas. For the most part, these are sponsored by banks, the major accountancy bodies, chambers of commerce, local or national newspapers, business magazines and the trade press. Government departments may also have their own competitions as a means of promoting their initiatives for exporting, innovation, job creation and so forth. There is a Business Plan Competition Directory on the Small Business Notes website, run by Judith Kautz (www.smallbusinessnotes.com/planning/competitions.html).

Jason and Katherine Salisbury started up their business, Suffolk Farmhouse Cheeses, in a renovated run-down cowshed next to their home. They bought second-hand equipment and, despite having two young children, have put in 18-hour days since going it alone in 2004. Their annual turnover is now £275,000 ($435,288) which they have financed in part with an £80,000 ($435,288) bank loan from HSBC. Now they are entering business competitions to fund expansion. They narrowly missed out on a £30,000 ($47,482) government grant in their first year of operations but since then have won through to the regional heats of HSBC's Start-up Stars Awards, from which they could win up to £25,000 ($39,579).

Cashless cash: using a local exchange trading scheme

Local exchange trading schemes (LETS) allow anyone who joins a scheme to offer skills or services, such as plumbing, gardening or the use of a photocopier, to other members. A price is agreed in whatever notional currency has been adopted, but no money changes hands. The system is more ambitious than straight barter. The provider receives a credit on their account, kept by a local organizer, and a debit is marked up against the user. The person in credit can then set this against other services.

The benefits of using LETS are that you can start trading and grow with virtually no start-up capital. All you need are time and saleable skills; once you have 'sold' your wares, payment is immediate by way of a LETS credit. Also, using LETS means that the wealth is kept in the local community, which means customers in your area may be able to spend more with you. One of the keys to success in using LETS is to have an enterprising organizer who can produce, maintain and circulate a wide-ranging directory of LETS services and outlets. Find out more about the system and how to find your nearest organizer from Letslink UK (www.letslinkuk.net).

Borrow from family and friends

Those close to you might be willing to lend you money or invest in your business, perhaps on better terms and at a lower cost that you would have to incur using more traditional financing routes. This helps you avoid the problem of pleading your case to outsiders and enduring extra paperwork and bureaucratic delays. Help from friends, relatives and business associates can be especially valuable if you have been through bankruptcy or had other credit problems that would make borrowing from a commercial lender difficult or impossible.

The involvement of family and friends brings a range of extra potential benefits, costs and risks that are not a feature of most other types of finance. You need to decide which of these are acceptable.

Some advantages of borrowing money from people you know well are that you may be charged a lower interest rate, may be able to delay paying back money until you are more established, and may be given more flexibility if you get into a jam. But once the loan terms are agreed to, you have the same legal obligations as you would with a bank or any other source of finance.

In addition, borrowing money from relatives and friends can have a major disadvantage. If your business does poorly and those close to you end up losing money, you may well damage a good personal relationship. So, in dealing with friends, relatives and business associates, be extra careful not only to establish clearly the terms of the deal and put them in writing, but also to make an extra effort to explain the risks. In short, it is your job to make sure your helpful friend or relative will not suffer true hardship if you are unable to meet your financial commitments.

Hippychick

When new mother Julie Minchin discovered the Hipseat she knew she had found a helpful product. Anything that makes carrying a baby around all day without ending up with excruciating backache has to be a benefit. It was only later that she realized that selling the product for the German company that made the Hipseat could be the right product to launch her into business. At first Julie acted as their UK distributor but later she wanted to make some major improvements to the product. That meant finding a manufacturer to make the product especially for her business. China was the logical place to find a company flexible enough to make small quantities as well as being able to help her keep the cost of the end product competitive.

She funded the business with a small family loan, an overdraft facility and a variety of grants secured with the help of Business Link. Now in its 10th year, the company has annual turnover of £3 million ($5 million) and sells 14 new and unique products aimed at the baby market. It supplies national chains such as Boots, Mothercare and Blooming Marvellous, as

well as independents. It also sell via its catalogue and website, and is in the
process of building a network of distributors for its branded products.

Get better terms from banks

Banks are the principal, and frequently the only, source of finance
for 9 out of 10 businesses. Firms big and small around the world
rely on banks for a very large proportion of their funding. In the
UK, for example, businesses have borrowed nearly £55 billion
($92 billion) from banks. That's not to say that getting a loan
is easy. As with any commodity, violent swings in price and
availability are the norm. In any 10 years you can expect bankers
to be shovelling cash in every direction for two or three years,
then pulling up the drawbridge for about the same length of time
during a credit squeeze; for the most part, though, reasonably
normal conditions will prevail.

Everything in business finance is negotiable, and your relationship with a bank is no exception. What's at stake is your ability to
negotiate an interest rate as close to the bank base rate as possible.
A premium of a quarter to half a percent over the prevailing base
rate might be considered satisfactory for a public company, whilst
a small private firm could pay anything from 3 per cent to 9 per
cent. Banks are in competition too, so if yours is being unreasonably hard, it may be time to move on. Even during the worst
credit crunch this century banks had to compete for business.
In July 2009 when things looked black for those in the buy-to-let
and property-development business sectors, the Bank of China,
Handelsbanken of Sweden, and Israel's Leumi began undercut-
ting the UK high street banks when the latter remained reluctant
to lend. The Bank of China had by then already put a toe in the
water in the commercial leasing sector.

Obviously, to be able to move on or get bank costs down, you
need to have some advance notice of when the additional funds
are needed. Rushing into a bank asking for extra finance from

next week is hardly likely to inspire much confidence in your abilities as a strategic thinker. It helps if you understand what a bank is looking at when it sets its terms.

Negotiating with bankers

Bankers like to speak of the 'five Cs' of credit analysis, factors they look at when they evaluate a loan request. When applying to a bank for a loan, be prepared to address the following points:

- Character. Bankers lend money to borrowers who appear honest and who have a good credit history. Before you apply for a loan, it makes sense to obtain a copy of your credit report and clean up any problems.
- Capacity. This is a prediction of the borrower's ability to repay the loan. For a new business, bankers look at the business plan. For an existing business, they consider financial statements and industry trends. You should have sufficient factual information to hand that shows your business sector in as favourable a light as possible.
- Collateral. Bankers generally want a borrower to pledge an asset that can be sold to pay off the loan if the borrower lacks funds. This may even call for the directors to give personal guarantees. This rather goes against the spirit of limited liability but can help with getting costs down. If you have to go this route, secure the guarantee against specific assets only and set clear conditions for the guarantee to come to an end, for example when your overdraft or borrowings return to the level they were at before your most recent request for additional funds. Otherwise the bank may try to retain the extra comfort of the security of a personal guarantee as part of your permanent banking arrangements.
- Capital. Bankers scrutinize a borrower's net worth, the amount by which assets exceed debts.

- Conditions. Whether bankers give a loan will be influenced by the current economic climate as well as by the amount. The economic climate that matters most is that which affects your business and the strategy you will be using the loan to implement. A well-prepared business plan will prove invaluable here.

Finding a business banker

You can see a listing of business bank account providers at Find.co.uk, the finance website (www.find.co.uk>Banking> Commercial>Business Banking), where the top six or so are star rated and reviewed, as well as an A–Z listing. Move Your Account (www.moveyouraccount.co.uk>Business Banking) offers a free service claiming to find you the best current banking deal. You have to complete a dozen questions online and await its response. Startups (www.startups.co.uk>Finance management>Business bank accounts) offers a range of advice and tips on opening or changing a business bank account and what charges to look out for. The British Banking Association (www.bba.moneyfacts.co.uk) has a business bank account finder tool that also lets you compare your present bank against any others you may choose.

Worldwide-Tax (www.worldwide-tax.com/banks/bankssites. asp) provides a directory to world banks and credit sites, sorted by country, and includes the major local and international banks that have branches in that country.

Putting spare cash to work

If there are stages in the month or year when you have surplus cash, putting it to work will have the effect of reducing your financing costs. Check out MaxBips (www.maxbips.com), launched in 2009. This is an auction-powered, real-time marketplace for term deposits. Depositors specify amount and term, and banks bid with interest rates. Anything from £30,000 ($50,000) available for 30 days or more can be put up for auction. There is a calculator on the site to provide an idea of what you would have paid the previous day for a given sum borrowed over periods up to 720 days.

Reduce the tax take

Governments around the world take a large share of business profits and in some cases that share is getting larger still. This is in part to deal with fallout from the global financial meltdown that started in 2007–08, and in part a wealth-redistribution agenda held to be important by most left-leaning regimes. The taxes that directly impinge on trading costs are taxes on profits and sales, also known as value-added taxes.

The position with regard to tax is changing more rapidly than at any time in recent financial history. The spill-over from the credit crunch that came to a head in 2008–09 has seen major changes to tax rates, VAT and writing-down allowances. In response to the unusually difficult trading climate in 2009 the UK government also allowed businesses to offset trading losses against tax already paid. The web address of H M Revenue & Customs, from which you can get current tax, VAT, national insurance and other business taxes, is given later in the chapter.

Keeping more profit

Tax on profits is often a business's biggest single expense, slicing anything from 20 to 40 per cent off the bottom line. All money that goes in taxes can be considered a waste as far as a business is concerned, as, unlike individuals who may see something of value for their tax, a business gets nothing back. So the rule here is to minimize tax within the law. The big companies have this down to a fine art: the top 700 UK companies paid no tax at all in 2008–09. These are some strategies for reducing taxes and so increasing retained profit, though some of that profit may not then be available as cash to the business:

- Check that you have charged all the allowable business expenses against profit. Bytestart.co.uk has a useful Business Expenses Guide (www.bytestart.co.uk >Money & Tax > Business Expenses Guide).
- Top up or start a pension, as you can put in up to £215,000 ($208,000) of your profits if you are a sole trader or in a partnership and so avoid paying up to £86,000 ($142,000) of tax. The rules for companies are more complex and potentially more tax efficient. If you take out a SIPPS (Self-invest personal pension scheme), you can invest the proceeds in most types of business premises, a shop, warehouse, office or workshop. Before you take the plunge, get professional advice from a tax expert and a pension provider. To find out more about SIPPS, you could contact the Pensions Advisory Service (TPAS), an independent non-profit organization and a good place to head for general information (www.opas.org.uk; 0845 601 2923); the Association of Independent Financial Advisors (www.aifa.net; 0207 628 1287); and the directory of UK tax professionals at TaxationWeb (www.taxationweb.co.uk/directory).
- Take advantage of your spouse's tax position, particularly if they have no other income from employment and are in a lower tax bracket than you.
- Invest in new equipment; anything designated as energy saving or that reduces water use currently qualifies for a 100 per cent tax allowance.

Value-added tax and sales tax

Value-added tax, known as VAT in Europe and as sales tax in the United States, is paid each quarter, but some businesses can take advantage of a number of schemes to simplify and so cut the cost of procedures or aid their cash flow. The annual accounting scheme lets you pay monthly or quarterly estimated figures, submitting a single annual return at the end of the year with any balancing payment. The cash accounting scheme allows you to delay handing over any VAT until you have actually collected it from your customers. This has the effect of reducing a firm's working capital, which in turn reduces the cost of any borrowings. The flat-rate scheme allows you to calculate your VAT as a flat percentage of your total sales, rather than having to record the VAT charged on individual purchases and sales. There are also schemes aimed at retailers, tour operators and those selling second-hand goods. H M Revenue & Customs (www.hmrc.gov.uk/vat/start/schemes/basics.htm) has information on the schemes and their likely cost advantages.

Walking the thin red line

The opportunities for cost cutting in the area of taxes are endless: from the seemingly prudent Marks & Spencer seeking to obtain group tax relief in respect of losses incurred by certain European subsidiary companies in Belgium, France and Germany, to the plain criminal: stuffing the business with false invoices. (China has the dubious distinction of being the world capital of false invoicing. In one year alone police there investigated 3,511 cases involving issuing false or tax-offsetting invoices, arrested 2,979 suspects, confiscated 10,510,000 fake invoices, smashed 101 illegal invoice-printing operations and retrieved 9.2 billion yuan (£640 million, $1,067 million) in under-declared taxes.)

The challenge for directors and business owners is to recognize the distinction between different types of behaviour when it comes to tax law:

■ Tax fraud, often called tax evasion to soften the underlying meaning, involves intentional behaviour or actual knowledge of wrongdoing: for example, reducing the tax burden by under-reporting income, overstating deductions, or using illegal tax shelters; this is a criminal matter.

- Tax mitigation involves the taxpayer taking advantage of a fiscally attractive option afforded by tax legislation and 'genuinely suffers the economic consequences that Parliament intended to be suffered by those taking advantage of the option', as one law lord summed the subject up. So for example, if a business is allowed to offset the cost of an asset against tax, then so long as they actually buy the asset they are mitigating their tax position.
- Tax avoidance lies in the blurred line between tax mitigation and tax fraud and is usually defined by the test of whether your dominant or sole purpose was to reduce or eliminate tax liability.

You must keep sufficient business records and paperwork for at least six years from the end of your company's accounting period, as the relevant authorities reserve the right to re-examine your accounts even if they have been approved. Take professional advice before taking major measures to cut tax costs.

Accountancy and audit

If you are a big business operating globally, you will have to have your accounts audited, and you will have little choice as to who carries out the audit. Only four accountancy firms offer a truly global audit service and a further score or so offer a reasonable approximation through a network of collaborators. For the remaining businesses that have to be audited, that is, those with a turnover above circa £5 million ($8.3 million), assets of around £3 million ($5 million) or shareholders who own more than 10 per cent of a firm, there are literally hundreds of thousands of firms that could carry out the task.

Entrepreneurs rarely see much value in the audit process. KPMG, one of the big-four auditors, recently surveyed 200 firms to canvas their views. Fifty-six per cent of those surveyed saw the audit as a routine chore and only 40 per cent of companies agreed that the audit raises issues and learning points that are useful for the business.

Generally cost will be a crucial factor for a private business in appointing an auditor, unless they are looking specifically to create a degree of external respectability: for example, if they are preparing to go public or raise large sums of new capital. Auditors have to be members of the major professional accounting bodies. You can keep track of who's who in the auditing world through *Accountancy Age* magazine (www.accountancyage.com/resource/top50), which lists the major audit firms in rank order each year. Pick a handful near you or, better still, get some recommendations from cost-conscious peers and negotiate for a much-reduced audit fee.

Cost-cutting assignment 6

Go back over this chapter and look for ways to cut the financing costs associated with operating your business.

1 Are there any sources of free money you could tap into?
2 Could you get a better deal from your bank?
3 Should you consider finding another bank?
4 Are your audit costs in line with those for comparable companies, and in any event should you be getting alternative quotes, looking for a better deal?
5 Are there periods of the year when you have surplus cash and if so, what do you do with that money, and could you do better?
6 Could you change your VAT/sales tax payment method to one more advantageous to your needs?
7 Are you taking all legal steps to minimize tax?

Cutting costs in a crisis

- Pruning pay;
- Killing finance costs;
- Realizing cash from assets;
- Moving the low-tax haven;
- Getting born again.

August 2009 saw broadcaster ITV reporting full-year losses of £2.59 billion ($4.32 billion), a consequence of the collapse in advertising revenue brought about by the prevailing economic crisis. By the time it reported these figures the company had already cut 1,000 jobs, secured £155 million ($258 million) in cost savings and had its sights set on cutting a further £215 million ($358 million) from overheads in 2010. In fact, the company's advertising-revenue decline of 15 per cent was a little better than that of the market as a whole, which had slipped back 17 per cent. Nevertheless, Michael Grade, the outgoing chairman, felt the situation drastic enough to call for further action. He sold the Friends Reunited website to Scottish publisher D C Thompson, of Beano fame, for £25 million ($42 million), some £150 million ($250 million) less than ITV had paid for it four years earlier. Whilst able to cite this as a bad purchase by ITV's previous management, Grade left a poisoned chalice of his own for future management. Part of the cost savings was derived from making fewer original programmes, an expensive and time-consuming process, and buying in ready-made titles from elsewhere. That strategy meant the company would lose out on the all-important international revenue that would accrue in future years, as the title to those products belonged to others. Despite waiving its interim dividend, ITV's share price rose 1 per cent on announcing its losses. One broker, Lorna Tilbian, analyst for the broadcast sector at Numis, summed up the reason why: 'ITV has been our favourite "death or glory" recovery play.' The investment community liked Grade's crisis cost-cutting strategy.

.The previous chapters have examined ways to cut costs under relatively normal conditions. Those are times when the management have some leeway and are free to make choices. That is not always the case. There are times when either the economic climate or the sector you are in faces a serious, perhaps even calamitous, situation. The collapse of the UK-owned motor industry, when 1,270 British motor manufacturers with names such as Abbey, Austin, Morris, Standard, Riley, Wolseley, Zephyr, were swept under between 1894 and 1960, is one example. Only a handful of firms survived, including Morgan under private UK ownership, MG within China's Nanjing Automobile Group, and a few other firms subsumed into American, French, Japanese and German ownership. The credit crunch of 2007–10 was a period when even the largest banking enterprises took to the lifeboats.

In such times the niceties of strategy may have to give way to the expediencies of survival. This chapter offers some ways to improve your chances of getting into a lifeboat and still being around when the storm subsides.

Slashing the wages bill

The introduction to this book detailed research that demonstrates that savage redundancies can have a serious and adverse effect on a company's share price and so on the value of the enterprise to its shareholders. Better, however, to have some residual value than none at all.

Cull headcount

The people you always need in an organization are the front-line staff making and selling things. That's not to say the other employees are doing nothing of value, just that when push comes to shove you could live without them. Over periods of plenty, middle management is prone to expand much like middle-age spread. When famine strikes it may be necessary to cut hard and cut deep. A good example here is that of Tony Hayward, who identified up to 11 levels of decision making between senior management and front-line staff when he took over at BP in October 2007. By July 2009 this had been reduced to seven, cutting out many jobs that had been duplicated across different business units. BP achieved $2 billion (£1.2 billion) in savings and had another $1billion in sight for 2009–10.

Often the only time an organization can get the unions and politicians to accept enormous job cuts is in a downturn, so unsurprisingly this is one of the first weapons the CCCO draws on when the chips are down. BT cut 30,000 jobs over the two-year period to January 2010 and Ford, Chrysler and General Motors between then shed 200,000 jobs in response to the major recession of 2008–10.

Freeze hiring

Employee numbers are one of the major cost drivers, with an impact that spreads beyond the sheer numbers themselves. People need space, equipment, cars, computers, pensions, insurance, sick pay – the list goes on. Double, triple or even quadruple the basic pay and you are getting close to the true cost of people in an organization. If culling is not an option, the next-best thing is a complete freeze in hiring. As people stay with an employer for around six years you could shed 15 per cent of your workforce each year without the pain or cost of redundancy. The three rules here are:

- Be ruthless. There can be no exceptions if this approach is to be effective, so you must be prepared for some modest retraining and reorganization to achieve your goals with a different balance of staffing.

- Be informed. The turnover index, sometimes called the wastage rate, is the traditional formula used by human resource experts. The formula is calculated as the number of leavers in the year divided by the average number of employees that year, multiplied by 100, to give a percentage. So if a department employing an average of 80 people over the year loses 10 people, its wastage rate is 12.5 per cent. Although the wastage formula is simple to use it can be misleading. It doesn't tell you anything about the sort of people that are leaving. It is more useful to use the skill stability index, which takes the number of people who have been with you for one or more years in each key skill area as a proportion of the number of people you employ in those skills; multiply that figure by 100 to give a percentage.
- Be prepared. Take steps to retain key employees so they don't become part of your wastage figures. Train, motivate, reward and promote where possible. Also stripping out layers of hierarchy and letting people go should present lots of opportunities for job enrichment.

Lower the wage bill

Staff are much more amenable to changes in pay and conditions when the going gets seriously tough. These are some strategies that were implemented in the 2008–10 downturn, with some success:

- Introduce a shorter working week. This in effect is spreading the same amount of work around more people as a way to reduce the number of employees being 'let go'. In March 2009 workers at Jaguar Land Rover's manufacturing operations in Castle Bromwich and Halewood switched to a four-day week in exchange for the company's agreement that there would not be any compulsory redundancies for two years.
- Freeze pay. ITV froze pay for its senior employees earning over £60,000 ($100,000) a year in February 2009, in light of fast-falling advertising revenues. A below-inflation pay rise

was imposed on full-time employees earning more than £25,000 ($42,000).

- Cut pay. A study by the British Chambers of Commerce (BCC) carried out in April 2009 revealed that in their sample of 400 companies, 12 per cent were planning to cut pay. In October 2008 some 2,500 staff based at seven different JCB factories voted to take a £50-a-week pay cut ($83) and work a four-day week in order to prevent 350 colleagues losing their jobs. In June 2009 British Airways persuaded 6,940 of its 40,000 employees to volunteer for unpaid leave, part-time working or unpaid work, saving the company up to £10 million ($16.7 million).

- Sell holidays to the staff. Acco Brands Europe, the office-supply firm, launched a holiday-purchase scheme for its 500 UK employees in February 2009. Employees can buy between 2 and 10 extra days' holiday per year, on top of their normal annual leave. The benefit is offered via salary sacrifice, so employees save on tax and national insurance contributions (NICs), and Acco makes savings of up to 12.8 per cent on NICs, in addition to cutting payroll costs. A pilot scheme produced savings of £37,964 ($63,263) in payroll costs for the company in one quarter.

- Offer shares in lieu of pay. In June 2009 British Airways pilots voted to take a pay cut in exchange for company shares, in order to cut payroll costs at the airline. The pilots will take a wage cut of 2.61 per cent on their basic pay as well as a 20 per cent cut in flying-time allowances. These changes will generate £26 million ($43.3 million) of annual savings for British Airways, in exchange for which the pilots were given shares worth £13 million ($21.6 million) if certain company targets are achieved. The pilots have to hold these for the three years to June 2014, after which they can sell or hold as they wish.

- Reduce pension benefits. In July 2009 Marks & Spencer announced changes to its final-salary pension scheme and early-retirement arrangements in a bid to cut operating costs by between £175 million ($291.6 million) and £200 million

($333.3 million). Annual increases in pensionable pay for the 21,000 active members of the final-salary pension scheme was capped at 1 per cent, whilst those who joined the pension scheme before 1996 also face reduced early-retirement benefits.

Unfair dismissal

Even if the changes to pay and conditions you have in mind to help with cutting costs don't actually amount to redundancy, employees can interpret major changes as constructive dismissal. Although it's the handful of cases usually brought by City workers that grab the headlines, some 180,000 unfair or constructive-dismissal claims are filed with tribunals each year: 40,000 of these proceed to a hearing and just under half of those are won by the employee, with the average claim being settled for £5,000 ($8,332). Employers who have been through the process say that it's the stress and administrative burden rather than the settlement itself that are of greatest concern. You can find a list of fair reasons for dismissing an employee in Monster's Employment Law website (www.compactlaw.co.uk/monster/empf9.html).

Make asset savings

Aside from cutting back on non-core activities, there are a number of more fundamental changes that can be made to achieve big savings in fixed costs.

Sell off land

If you are sitting on land assets that you had set aside for a rainy day, then now is the time to realize any value, and pump that cash back into the business. British International Helicopters (see case study below) is an interesting example of killing several birds with one stone. Their move would cut operating costs whilst realizing a profit on the sale of valuable building land. The main losers would be customers who face an extra 30-minute car journey and some employees who would have to relocate.

British International Helicopters (BIH), Penzance

By December 2008, BIH's managing director Tony Jones was facing a dilemma. His company, based on the edge of Penzance and close to the main rail station and harbour, provides one of a number of vital links between the mainland and the Isles of Scilly. Annual passenger numbers had declined from 133,000 in 2002 to 100,000 in 2008, and the prospects for tourism in the credit-crunch environment that prevails in 2009–10 does not augur well. Along with the rising costs of spare parts and fuel, the service had been steadily becoming less viable over the previous four years. The company's operating profit has reduced by £1.2 million ($2 million) a year and something drastic has to be done to keep the business going and preserve the firm's 86 jobs.

Raising fares is not an option. Travelling by helicopter is already a costly, if convenient, option. BIH's standard fare of £170 ($283) for the 20-minute flight compares unfavourably both with Skybus's fixed-wing service at £140 ($233), available from Land's End aerodrome, some 30 minutes' drive away, and with the 2½-hour ferry crossing on the Scillonian for £95 ($158).

BIH's proposed recovery strategy involves selling off the Penzance Heliport, which is sandwiched between branches of Morrisons and Tesco on prime land on the edge of town, and transferring flights to the Land's End airport. As well as the fact that this would free up a substantial capital sum, BIH's operating costs would drop sharply, as it would be sharing the costs of running Land's End airport with Skybus, and its flying time (and hence fuel and operating costs) would be reduced significantly. Firefighters, baggage handlers and administrative staff would be transferred to Land's End but many staff would stay in or near the existing heliport. Passengers, however, would in effect be suffering a substantial rise in fares as they would have to foot the bill for a 30-minute taxi. However, this price hike would be less visible, as headline helicopter fares might appear unchanged. The environment looks like being a loser too, with more pollution, traffic and accidents.

Sell and lease back assets

Sale and leaseback are usually seen as a last resort only to be sub-scribed to in the most desperate of times. The process involves selling some or all of your property assets to another company and becoming a tenant in what were your premises. The benefits are a slug of cash to help ride out a storm, plus a way to reduce future operating costs as a tax benefit can be realized by offsetting lease costs as an operating expense. IBM, for example, sold and leased back four of its five remaining owned sites in the UK in 2006, leaving only its Hursley software laboratory in company ownership. As well as reducing costs, IBM is increasingly trying to have only sufficient property on the books to meet business demands; leasing on relatively short terms helps in this respect. Other big users of sale and leaseback include Tesco, who recently made a £366 million ($610 million) property sale and leaseback of 12 stores and two distribution centres.

Reduce financing and tax costs

Just as with pay and work conditions, recessions or crises are times when seemingly irreducible finance and tax costs can be slimmed down radically or eliminated altogether, for the time being at least.

Slash dividends

Even if your shareholders have been used to a big payout, now is the time to make them share the burden too. BT dramatically reduced its final 2009 dividend to 1.1p, down from 10.4p the year before, in an attempt to save cash. In that same year Sony halved its payout and Pfizer also cut its dividend by 50 per cent, sweet-ening this with a $68 billion (£41 billion) deal to buy drug maker Wyeth.

Negotiate a tax time-to-pay plan

H M Revenue & Customs (HMRC) has been induced to change its normally heartless stance and in 2009 alone allowed almost £2 billion ($3.3 billion) in personal and business taxes to be deferred in 110,000 separate agreements for those having difficulty meeting tax obligations. Those deferring tax payments are being offered better rates of interest than are generally available from commercial banks. Interest on tax outstanding is charged at 1.75 per cent, whilst for VAT, national insurance and capital gains tax the rate is 2.5 per cent. HMRC may consider allowing time to pay if requested by the taxpayer or their accountant and will use their telephone debt management skills to determine whether the customer is a 'can't pay' or a 'won't pay'. There is no simple rule of thumb for making this decision, so expect detailed questioning.

Relocate to a low-tax country

From 2010 the UK looks set to become a less attractive place in which to do business, from a tax perspective at least. High income tax, 50 per cent a near certainty, combined with limitations on high earners' tax-efficient pension contributions, has created a flurry of interest in relocating to a more benign tax environment. Most countries have some form of taxation and the rules are often different for foreigners who invest in the country. Business taxes vary widely around the world. The Maldives (9 per cent) and the United Arab Emirates (15 per cent) are towards the low end of the scale, whilst Italy (76 per cent) and India (81 per cent) are among countries with the highest business taxes. All business taxes are complicated, but in some countries they are more complicated than others. For example, it takes over 1,000 hours to prepare and file all business taxes in countries such as Ukraine, Brazil and the Czech Republic, yet in Singapore, Switzerland and the Seychelles the same task can be completed in under 70 hours.

Swap debt for equity

The attractions to share capital from a business's perspective are that it is risk free and dividends are, to a degree at least, optional. Banks are a bit less forgiving and expect interest payments to be made irrespective of performance. Companies big and not so big are using this emergency cost-cutting strategy, which usually involves diluting the holding of existing shareholders. Following are some of the companies that are making debt-for-equity swaps in the summer of 2009:

- Samsonite, the world's biggest maker of suitcases, backpacks and carry-bags ran into trouble and needed to be saved by swapping debt for equity. CVC Capital Partners, one of Europe's biggest private equity groups, has agreed to pay $175 million (£105 million) to retain a controlling 60 per cent stake in Samsonite, funds that will provide fresh capital for a US brand hit by the recent decline in international air travel. Royal Bank of Scotland, which is controlled by the UK government, took a minority stake in Samsonite in a deal that will cut Samsonite's debt from about $800 million (£480 million) to $240 million (£144 million).

- Ferretti, the Italian yacht maker, was taken over by its banks and management, wiping out the total investment of the existing shareholder, private equity group Candover.

- Polish meat producer Duda restructured its PLN301.2 million ($103.2 million, £62 million) debt through a debt-for-equity swap with Kredyt Bank.

- The Bay Restaurant Group, owner of the La Tasca and Slug and Lettuce chains, previously part of the Laurel Pub Company, agreed terms for a debt-for-equity swap with Icelandic bank Kaupthing and Germany's Commerzbank on a financial restructure that will reduce its debts by £150 million ($250 million). In 2008, two of the group's three brands, Slug and Lettuce, and ha ha bar and grill, were part of a pre-pack administration that divided the business into two: Bay Restaurants, and the Town and City Pub Company (for more on pre-packs, see Cobra Beer case study, below).

Cut and run

Business owners often resort to the desperate measures outlined above in an attempt to stay in business when the economic facts of life are all against them. Unfortunately, failure is a fact of business life, with over 400,000 businesses closing down each year in the UK alone. If handled properly, exiting from an unprofitable business can leave you in reasonable shape to start again. Sock Shop, the business founded in 1983 by Sophie Mirman, a former typist at Marks & Spencer, has closed down and reopened three times since then. Its latest incarnation in 2006 saw it mainly as a web-based business with just one 60 square metres outlet at Manchester Airport.

At the very least you should work within the law. These are the main options for closing down a business:

- Voluntary arrangements were brought into being by the Insolvency Act 1986. Until then it was not possible for a debtor to make a legally binding compromise with all their creditors. Any single creditor could scupper the plans. Now a debtor can make a proposal to their creditors to pay all or part of the debt over a period of time. The mechanics are simple. The debtor applies to the court for an interim order stating that they intend to make a proposal naming a qualified insolvency practitioner who will be advising them. The position is then frozen, preventing bankruptcy proceedings until the insolvency practitioner reports back to the court. A creditors' meeting will be called, notifying all creditors, and if the proposal is approved by more than 75 per cent by value of the creditors' meeting, it will be binding on all creditors.
- Receivership occurs when a borrower (a company) fails to meet its obligations to a mortgagee. The most usual scenario is where a company gives a charge over assets to its bankers. This in turn allows the banker to advance funds to the company. In these circumstances, if the company fails to meet its obligations to its bankers – for example by not repaying money when due – then the bank can appoint a receiver. The

receiver has wide powers to step in and run the business or sell off its assets for the benefit of the person who appointed the receiver. The existing directors' authority will be suspended and existing contracts with the company only have to be carried out by the receiver if the receiver believes it worthwhile to do so. Money generated by the receiver first goes to paying the costs of selling assets (auctioneers' fees), then to paying the receiver's own fees. Only then will the person appointing the receiver get their debt paid. Once that too has been discharged, others further down the pecking order, such as those holding preferential debts, may get paid.

■ Winding up and liquidation can be imposed on a limited company if it is considered to be unable to pay its debts and a creditor leaves a demand for a debt of £750 ($1,250) or more in a certain prescribed form at its registered office and that debt is not paid within 21 days. Once this position is reached an application can be made for the company to be wound up. The company itself can ask to be wound up, as can any creditor; in some circumstances various government officials can so ask. Before a winding-up order is made, the court appoints a provisional liquidator – always called 'the official receiver'. Once the winding-up order is made, all court proceedings against the company are stopped; all employees' contracts are terminated and its directors are dismissed. The liquidator's job is to get in the company's assets and pay off the creditors.

■ Administration is a way to help companies in serious financial difficulties to trade their way back to financial health. The thinking here is similar to that behind that voluntary arrangements, although administration usually involves much more substantial sums. Whilst in administration, the company is protected from its creditors whilst an approved rescue plan is implemented. Administration orders will only be made where the court is satisfied that the company has cash available from either shareholders or lenders to finance the rescue plan.

Cobra Beer

In 1990, Cambridge-educated and recently qualified accountant Karan Bilimoria started importing and distributing Cobra Beer, a name he chose because it appeared to work well in lots of different languages. He initially supplied his beer to complement Indian restaurant food in the UK. Lord Bilimoria, as he now is, started out with debts of £20,000 ($33,300), from a small flat in Fulham, and with just a Citroën CV by way of assets grew his business to sales of over £100 million a year. Bilimoria's extensive knowledge of sources of finance through his training as an accountant helped him tap into every possible type of funding.

However, in the summer of 2009, the credit crunch claimed him as yet another victim. Cobra folded with debts of almost £70 million ($116.6 million). Investors lost £57.3 million ($95.5 million), H M Revenue & Customs £6.4 million ($10.7 million) and a further £6 million ($10 million) was lost by some 330 unsecured creditors. Three small companies that had worked with Cobra – Spark Promotions and MicroMatic, who developed beer pumps, and Pop Display, who produced promotional material – were owed substantial five-figure sums, large enough to threaten their businesses with redundancies or worse.

Bilimoria emerged from this failure almost immediately as a director and 49.9 per cent shareholder of a new joint venture with an American brewer, running what is in essence the old Cobra Beer company. The process that facilitated the miracle resurrection was a pre-pack. In a pre-pack, a company is placed into administration and sold just a few days or in some cases hours after the appointment of the administrator. Frequently the insolvency practitioner, the directors and the bank will have agreed a sales price and drafted contracts to enable the business to be sold immediately after appointment. The Enterprise Act 2002, Administration* paved the way for this process and in September 2007 a judge in the High Court ruled in favour of using a pre-pack to save a business and the jobs of its 50-plus employees, against the wishes of the major creditor.

---

* Administration is a legal process that allows a company in financial difficulties to continue to trade while a plan is formulated to rescue the company or achieve a better deal for the creditors.

Falling foul of the authorities

Whilst cutting costs drastically, there are three types of activities that directors need to steer clear of if they don't want to join the thousand or so directors that are disqualified and fined each year, or the rather smaller number who end up at Her Majesty's pleasure for seven years or more. In addition, you can be made personally liable for the debts and liabilities of any company in which you are involved.

Disqualification means that not only can't you run a company but if you issue your orders through others, having them act as director(s) in your place, you will leave them personally liable themselves. You will also be in breach of a disqualification order that can in turn lead to imprisonment and fines.

Here are the three activities that are illegal:

- Trading whilst insolvent occurs when your liabilities exceed your assets. At this point the shareholders' equity in the business has effectively ceased to exist, and when shareholder equity is negative, directors are personally at risk and owe a duty of care to creditors rather than shareholders. If you find yourself even approaching this area you need the prompt advice of an insolvency practitioner. Directors who act properly will not be penalized, and will live to fight another day.
- Wrongful trading can apply if, after a company goes into insolvent liquidation, the liquidator believes that the directors (or those acting as such) ought to have concluded earlier that the company had no realistic chance of survival. In these circumstances the courts can remove the shelter of limited liabilities and make directors personally liable for the company's debts.
- Fraudulent trading is rather more serious than wrongful trading. Here the proposition is that the director(s) was or were knowingly party to fraud on their creditors. The full shelter of limited liability can be removed in these circumstances.

Cost-cutting assignment 7

Go back over this chapter and look for ways to cut costs radically and, if necessary, park the long view and focus on survival.

1 Are there staff that, though useful, you could live without for the next year or so? If so what would be the savings and consequences of releasing them?
2 Are there steps you can take to radically reduce your wages bill, say by asking people to take pay cuts, eliminate overtime or swap pay for shares?
3 Do you have assets you could sell and lease back?
4 Are there any business units or subsidiaries that you could sell off and still have a viable business?
5 Would anyone you have borrowed from or owe money to consider swapping that debt for shares in the business?
6 Do you owe H M Revenue & Customs for tax, and should you talk to them about getting time to pay?
7 Is there somewhere else to relocate to where your cost base would be lower?
8 Should you be talking to your accountant about putting in place a plan to liquidate and start again (a pre-pack)?

8
Staying lean and mean

- Setting cost budgets;
- Benchmarking standards;
- Setting priorities;
- Motivating cost cutters;
- Staying the course.

Cost cutting is not a one-off process just to deal with a cash-flow crisis or to ensure survival in the face of an extraordinary set of events. You can think of costs as a form of financial flab that has to be worked on constantly if an organization is to prosper and endure. Cost-cutting budgets need to be prepared, performance reviewed and plans implemented. The CCCO's task is a lifetime's work and they need to harness the energies of everyone in the organization to that end.

Budget for cuts

Budgeting is the principal management tool to ensure that objectives are set and met and that costs are monitored and controlled. They are not set in stone, since circumstances change. In the words of John Maynard Keynes, the famous economist: 'When the facts change, I change my mind.' Budgets are usually reviewed at least halfway through the year and often quarterly. At that review a further quarter or half year can be added to the budget to maintain a one-year budget horizon. This is known as a 'rolling quarterly (half-yearly) budget'.

Forecasting

Sales drive much of a business's activities; they determine cash flow, stock levels, production capacity and ultimately how profitable or otherwise a business will be. So, unsurprisingly, much of a cost cutter's effort needs to go into attempting to predict future sales. A sales forecast is not the same as a sales objective. An objective is what you want to achieve and will shape a strategy to do so. A forecast is the most likely future outcome given what has happened in the past and the momentum that provides for the business.

Forecasts are made up of three components, and to get an accurate forecast you need to decompose the historical data to better understand the impact of each on the end result:

■ Underlying trend. This is the general direction, up, flat or down, over the longer term, showing the rate of change. You can fit a trend line by eye or by using a mathematical technique. The trend tells you something about future resource requirements.

■ Cyclical factors. These are the short-term influences that regularly superimpose themselves on the trend. For example, in the summer months you would expect sales of certain products – such as swimwear, ice cream and suntan lotion – to be higher than in winter. Ski equipment would probably follow a reverse pattern. Understanding these seasonal movements is essential for forecasting short-term cash-flow needs and so minimizing the cost of working capital.

■ Random movements. These are irregular random spikes up or down, caused by unusual and unexplained factors. There is nothing much you can do about these except to look at past data and see how large and frequent these spikes have been in the past, so you have some idea of what to be prepared for.

Cost-budget principles

The forecast is the most reliable starting point for deciding on the cost structure of the budget. Surprisingly few CFOs make forecasts, preferring instead to start by building their entire budget on the objectives alone. The test as to whether or not those objectives are realistic and achievable to a large extent depends on the gap between the trend and the objective. For example, if sales of a product, division or business unit have been growing at 10 per cent a year for the past few years, you would need a pretty convincing argument to persuade you to build a cost budget around an objective that called for 25 per cent growth.

Budgets should adhere to the following general principles:

- The budget must be based on realistic but challenging goals. These are arrived at by both a top-down 'aspiration' of senior management and a bottom-up forecast of what the department concerned sees as possible.
- The budget should be prepared by those responsible for delivering the results: the salespeople should prepare the sales budget and the production people the production budget. Senior managers must maintain the communication process so that everyone knows what other parties are planning for.
- Agreement to the budget should be explicit. During the budgeting process, several versions of a particular budget should be discussed. For example, the boss may want costs reduced by £2 million ($3.3 million), but the business team's initial forecast is for £1.75 million ($2.9 million). After some debate, £1.9 million ($3.14 million) may be the figure agreed upon. Once a figure is agreed, a virtual contract exists that declares a commitment from employees to achieve the target and commitments from the employer to be satisfied with the target and to supply resources in order to achieve it. It makes sense for this contract to be in writing.
- The budget needs to be finalized at least a month before the start of the year and not weeks or months into the year.

- The budget should undergo fundamental reviews periodically throughout the year to make sure all the basic assumptions that underpin it still hold good.
- Accurate information with which to review performance against budgets should be available 7 to 10 working days before the month's end.

Demonstrated best practice (benchmarking)

One way to get a feel for how to set cost-improvement targets in a budget is to see what the best companies in your sector are achieving. If, for example, an admired competitor is getting its audit carried out for £5,000 ($8,500) and yours is costing £20,000 ($33,000), that information would represent a potential cost saving. Similarly, if the best companies are achieving 50 per cent gross profit and you are only getting 45 per cent, that would be an area to probe.

Following are the key sources of financial performance and relative cost structures that the well-informed CCCO should draw on when setting cost-improvement budgets:

- Companies House (www.companieshouse.gov.uk) is the official repository of all company information in the UK. Their WebCheck service offers a free searchable company names and addresses index that covers 2 million companies either by name or by each company's unique company registration number.
- FAME (Financial Analysis Made Easy) is a powerful database that contains information on 3.4 million companies in the UK and Ireland. You can compare each company's detailed financials with those of its peer group based on its activity codes, and the software lets you search for companies that comply with your own criteria, combining as many conditions as you like. FAME is available in business libraries and on CD from the publishers, who also offer a free trial (www. bvdep.com/en/companyInformationHome.html>Company data – national > FAME).

■ Free Company Reports and Accounts (www.fcreports.com) is an online service offering free instant downloads of financial reports from listed companies in the UK. Annual reports, balance sheets, profit and loss statements and interim reports are available from one of the largest databases of listed companies in the UK.

■ Keynote (www.keynote.co.uk) operates in 18 countries, providing business ratios and trends for 140 industry sectors, with information to assess accurately the financial health of each sector. Using this service you can find out how profitable a business sector is and how successful the main companies operating in each sector are. Executive summaries are free, but expect to pay between £250 ($417) and £500 ($834) for most reports.

Variance analysis

Explaining variances is also a CCCO-type task, so performance needs to be carefully monitored and compared against the budget as the year proceeds, and corrective action must be taken where necessary. This has to be done on a monthly basis (or using shorter time intervals if required), showing both the company's performance during the month in question and throughout the year so far. The more frequently costs are reviewed, the more opportunities there are to keep on track.

Looking at Table 8.1, we can see at a glance that the business is behind on sales for this month, but ahead on the yearly target. The convention is to put all unfavourable variations in brackets. Hence, a higher-than-budgeted sales figure does not have brackets, whilst a higher materials cost does. We can also see that, whilst profit is running ahead of budget, the profit margin is slightly behind (−0.30 per cent). This is partly because other direct costs, such as labour and distribution in this example, are running well ahead of budget.

Table 8.1 The fixed-cost budget

Heading	Month			Year to date		
	Budget	Actual	Variance	Budget	Actual	Variance
Sales	805*	753	(52)	6,358	7,314	956
Materials	627	567	60	4,942	5,704	(762)
Materials margin	178	186	8	1,416	1,610	194
Direct costs	74	79	(5)	595	689	(94)
Gross profit	104	107	3	820	921	101
Percentage	**12.92**	**14.21**	**1.29**	**12.90**	**12.60**	**(0.30)**

* Figures indicate thousands of pounds

Flexing the budget

A budget is based on a particular set of goals, few of which are likely to be exactly met in practice. Table 8.2 shows a company that has used £762,000 ($1,270,000) more materials than budgeted. As more has been sold, this is hardly surprising. The way to manage this situation is to flex the budget to show what would be expected to happen to expenses, given the sales that actually

Table 8.2 The flexed budget

Heading	Month			Year to date		
	Budget	Actual	Variance	Budget	Actual	Variance
Sales	753*	753	–	7,314	7,314	–
Materials	587	567	20	5,685	5,704	(19)
Materials margin	166	186	20	1,629	1,610	(19)
Direct costs	69	79	(10)	685	689	(4)
Gross profit	97	107	10	944	921	(23)
Percentage	**12.92**	**14.21**	**1.29**	**12.90**	**12.60**	**(0.30)**

* Figures indicate thousands of pounds

occurred. Applying the budget ratios to the actual data does this. For example, materials were planned to be 22.11 per cent of sales in the budget. By applying that to the actual month's sales, a materials cost of £587,000 ($958,000) is arrived at.

Looking at this flexed budget, we can see that the company has spent £19,000 ($31,700) more than expected on materials, given the level of sales actually achieved, rather than the £762,000 overspend shown in the fixed budget.

The same principle holds for other direct costs, which appear to be running £94,000 ($157,000) over budget for the year. When we take into account the extra sales shown in the flexed budget, we can see that the company has actually spent £4,000 ($6,700) over budget on direct costs. Whilst this is serious, it is not as serious as the fixed budget suggests.

The flexed budget allows you to concentrate your efforts on dealing with true variances in cost performance.

The website SCORE (www.score.org > Business Tools > Template Gallery > Sales Forecast) has a downloadable Excel spreadsheet from which you can make sales and cost projections on a trial-and-error basis. Once you are satisfied with your projection, use the profit and loss projection (www.score.org > Business Tools > Template Gallery > Profit and Loss Projection (3 Years)) to complete your budget.

Seasonality and trends

The figures shown for each period of the budget are not the same. For example, a sales budget of £1.2 million ($2 million) for the year does not translate to £100,000 ($167,000) a month. The exact figure depends on two factors:

■ The projected trend may forecast that, whilst sales at the start of the year are £80,000 ($133,000) a month, they will change to £120,000 ($200,000) a month by the end of the year. The average would be £100,000 ($167,000).

■ By virtue of seasonal factors, each month may also be adjusted up or down from the underlying trend. You could expect the sales of heating oil, for example, to peak in the autumn and tail off in the late spring.

Zero-base budgets

When you sit down with your team and discuss budgets, the arguments always revolve around how much more each section will need next year. The starting point is usually this year's costs, which are taken as the only facts upon which to build. So, for example, if you spent £50,000 ($83,000) on advertising last year and achieved sales of £2 million ($3.33 million), your advertising expense was 2.5 per cent of sales. If the sales budget for next year is £4 million ($6.66 million), then it seems logical to spend £100,000 ($166,000) next year on advertising. That, however, presupposes that last year's sum was wisely and effectively spent in the first place, which it almost certainly was not.

Zero-base budgeting turns the cost argument on its head. It assumes that each year every cost centre starts from zero spending and, based on the goals of the business and the resources available, arguments are presented for every pound or dollar to be spent, not just for the increase.

Set cost-cutting priorities

The budget sets the overall cost goals for the organization. However, you still have to decide the precise actions that will enable you to achieve the savings and the order in which those actions will be executed. Clearly you can't do everything at once, so it makes sense to prioritize the tasks ranked in some way that recognizes that not all actions are equally easy to carry out, nor do they have equal cost-savings potential.

Figure 8.1 provides a framework to help with such decisions by ranking actions using two basic criteria: the ease or difficulty

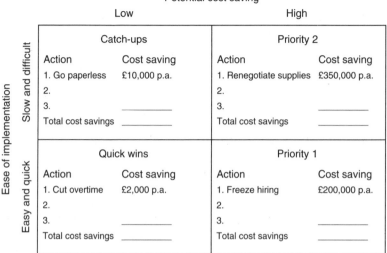

Figure 8.1 Setting cost-savings priorities

of carrying out the task; and the likely savings to be achieved once the task is accomplished. This example shows that some sizeable savings can be accomplished quickly by freezing hiring, which puts it in the priority 1 quadrant. Renegotiating with suppliers could make even larger savings, but these will take time as the business has contracts to unwind, making this a candidate for the priority 2 quadrant. Cutting overtime is labelled a quick win, as it is easy to implement, but doesn't reduce costs significantly. Quick wins can be implemented alongside Priority 1 tasks, or at any stage that morale-boosting savings are needed to reassure managers that cost-cutting targets can be met, or when political signals are required, for example to demonstrate to shareholders that a cost-saving programme is under way. The savings from quick wins are usually too small to spend much time on, but can prove valuable nevertheless. The final quadrant, headed catch-ups, comprises difficult tasks that won't reduce costs by much, and should be left to last.

The examples given are just that, and the cost-savings strategies that matter most to one business might be totally irrelevant to another: so too with the ease of implementation. British Airways, for example, found it relatively easy to discuss the idea of changing salary for share options with their pilots as many already owned shares and were familiar with the risks and potential rewards of ownership. BT would perhaps not find that as easy a cost-savings concept to sell to its repair staff.

Making cost cuts happen

Setting a budget and allocating priorities, whilst necessary parts of the cost-cutting process, are insufficient in themselves to make the savings a reality. To achieve this requires that as many people as possible in the organization are motivated and rewarded for achieving those goals. This involves moving people and the organization from a position of relative comfort to a state of accepting that the changes required to implement strategic cost cutting is the new steady state. The story often told to illustrate the dangers of ignoring the need for this change is that of the hypothetical frog dropped into a pot of boiling water. The immediate impact of a radically different environment spurs the frog into action, so that it leaps out of the pot. The same frog placed in the same pot, but in which the initial temperature is much lower, will allow itself to be boiled to death: it fails to recognize the danger if the process is slow enough.

Managing the cost-cutting process

Because the changes required by cost cutting are inevitable and unpredictable in their consequences doesn't mean that it can't be managed as a process. These are the stages in managing change, which, if followed, will give you a better chance of success in achieving a long-term cost-cutting programme.

Tell them why

Cost cutting is better accepted when people are given a compelling business reason. Few bankers would question the need for a radical review of costs and business structures after the 2008 debacles at Bear Stearns, SocGen and Northern Rock. Here are a couple of the arguments that will strike a chord with most managers and employees:

- Uncertain economic times. This is a fact of business life, so businesses need to always be run as if a serous recession was just weeks away. The idea that business cycles in general and boom-and-bust economic conditions in particular had been banished was a relatively popular view held by, among others, Gordon Brown when he was Chancellor of the Exchequer. This complacent view was encouraged by a record uninterrupted period of prosperity and stability referred to as the 'great moderation'. Politicians reckoned they had the business cycle beaten. Business cycles, as it turns out, are not only not banished, they are as difficult as ever to predict with any degree of accuracy when it comes to timing or severity. The world economic crisis that started in 2008 came out of a clear blue sky with few storm clouds in sight. Central bankers in the developed economies were talking of the prospects for a 'soft landing' and of the reasonable prospects of avoiding a recession as late as the spring of 2008. By the autumn of 2008 the UK Chancellor declared the economy was in the midst of the worst economic storm in 60 years, a period now being compared with the Great Depression that started in 1929. Although the warning is likely to be short, businesses should always be prepared for downturns and cautious of being swept up in the excitement of booms.
- Competitive pressures. Use the information on competitors' performance to demonstrate the necessity of changing cost behaviour. The information gathered in the benchmarking process should prove a rich source of arguments for accepting cost cuts. If, for example, companies in your sector have

a higher gross margin, lower operating costs and fewer employees per dollar or pound of sales generated, these represent compelling arguments to present to managers and employees alike.

Sell the green vision

Over the past decade, the business community has experienced what amounts to a green revolution. Pressures on business abound for them to produce less waste, use less energy, consume less water, encourage employees to walk or cycle or to work from home for at least part of the time. That this green wave has received the enthusiastic support of business is in large measure because many of these activities are consistent with aggressive long-term cost cutting. The beauty, from a business perspective, is that this pressure to go green comes from outside and is supported in many cases by legislation. Companies such as 3M, DuPont, IBM and latterly Google, Cisco and Microsoft are enthusiastic green cost cutters and have saved billions. Toyota with innovative hybrids such as the Prius, have created what amounts to new streams of revenue whilst greatly enhancing the value of their brand.

The evidence is that employees like working for green businesses. A global study by Hill & Knowlton, the corporate communications firm, revealed that 4 in every 10 MBA students would not take 'a great offer' from a company with a poor environmental reputation. Another survey covering college students found that 92 per cent want to work for a green company. Ray Anderson, founder and CEO of Interface Flooring, has reduced energy and waste costs by hundreds of millions of dollars in cost-savings programmes. But Anderson claims an equally important benefit for going green: 'In my 51 years in business, I've never seen an issue galvanize people in a company like sustainability.' Interface believes sustainability presents a strategic opportunity to build value by driving reputation and cost reductions.

Make cost cutting manageable

Even when people accept what needs to be done, the change may just be too big for anyone to handle. Breaking it down into manageable bits can help overcome this problem. The phrase 'eating your elephant a bite at a time' springs to mind here.

Use the framework in Figure 8.2 to break the total cost-cutting objective into smaller units of activity that can be spread more thinly around the organization.

Take a shared approach

Involve people early, asking them to join you in managing cost cutting, and give key participants some say in shaping events right from the start. This will reduce the feeling that change is being imposed, and more brains will be brought to bear on the problem.

Use smart circles

One entrepreneur who has built his company to a £3 million ($5.7 million) business from a standing start five years earlier formed his 20 employees into what he called smart circles. He challenged them to find ways the firm could do things faster, better and at a lower cost. In year one he doubled profits and within five years his business was valued at £10 million ($16.7 million).

The key to success with such initiatives is to build the teams across functions, keep them small and set some work time and space for them to meet. Keep formalities to the minimum, but insist on a team leader being appointed and brief reports prepared. Change the team composition several times a year and publicize successes.

Health Aid

Joshua Kirkham started his company, Health Aid, to produce and market Nebulizers, a device that helps asthmatics recover quickly from an attack. Basically the device consists of a pump that forces a drug into the sufferer's lungs. The product was specifically tailored to the needs of older people with asthma, who surprisingly were not being offered a suitable nebulizer. The only products then on the market were aimed at children, but for the adult market a more powerful pump was required.

The company quickly grew to £1 million ($1.67 million) turnover per annum, employing some 16 people. Although turnover had grown, profits had stabilized and the firm was having difficulty in keeping its shopfloor workers. They operated in a prosperous area, where employment was high and new firms were setting up all the time. Joshua decided to tackle the profit issues first. With all his employees he took a detailed look at everything they did, with a view to increasing the profitability of every hour they worked. Each process was examined and made the subject of a brainstorming session. For example, one part of the manufacturing process of their nebulizer products required several hundred plastic parts to be tipped onto a table. Invariably 50 or so fell off the table and were either damaged or took valuable seconds to recover. By putting a three-inch-high plastic rim around the table, at a cost of £5 ($8.30) the company saved two hours' production time per week. Several hundred simple ideas like this reduced the total production time for one key product by nearly 40 per cent.

The overall effect was quite staggering. At long last Health Aid managed to grow both profit and sales. Profitability got progressively better and within 12 months the company was making six times as much profit as before. Interestingly, fewer people left the firm that 12 months than ever before.

Institute a suggestion scheme

Founded in 1987, ideasUK is a not-for-profit association in the UK dedicated to the development of efficient and effective staff-suggestion schemes. Their thousand or so members and award winners include companies and organizations such as Boots, Bupa, Center Parcs, Charity Commission, Diageo, Emirates Airline, GlaxoSmithKline and the Ministry of Defence.

To get the best out of a scheme, follow these basic guidelines:

- New suggestion schemes must be carefully planned and provided with the resources and management backing to sustain them over the long term. There are a lot of dead schemes around; they die very quickly if they are not properly run.
- Schemes require constant promotion. Memories are short and as soon as you stop talking about the scheme suggestions will dry up.
- Schemes should be fun. They can be enlivened with short-term campaigns aimed at encouraging suggestions in areas such as energy saving, the environment or low-cost customer care. League tables, a lucky dip from a tub of accumulated suggestions or a boss's prize for the best of the year can all sustain interest.
- Suggestions must be handled quickly and efficiently. If employees have an idea and get excited, they should not be kept waiting more than 24 hours for an acknowledgement, and you should come up with a response to the suggestion within a week.
- Suggestions should be rewarded, usually by giving 'little and often'. On average, schemes pay out about a fifth of the savings.

Reward success early

According to a recent survey by Harris Interactive and Ranstad USA, 93 per cent of employees turn off lights, TVs and other electrical equipment to conserve energy before they leave home, but only 50 per cent do the same when leaving work. Some 77 per cent of employees recycle at home whilst only 49 per cent do so at the office. According to the researchers, the reasons lie in the fact that there is no benefit for them in saving business costs and in any event their small effort in a workforce of hundreds or thousands is unlikely to be noticed.

To get round this, flag up cost-cutting successes as quickly as possible; don't wait for the year end or the appraisal cycle. This will inspire confidence and keep the cost-cutting process on track.

Build in rewards, perhaps little more than simply giving employees credit for their achievements and praise in some public manner. Interface Flooring (see above), in a partnership with Ashridge Business School, have established InterfaceRAISE, a peer-to-peer advisory service for businesses to show how Interface have applied sustainability as a cost reducer and growth platform in the best and worst of times. This is a very public opportunity for their employees to gain recognition for their green achievements. Not only does that cost Interface nothing, they actually sell the advice to Ashridge clients.

Expect resistance

Kurt Lewin, a German-born professor at the Massachusetts Institute of Technology, was one of the first researchers to study group dynamics and how change can be best effected in organizations. In 1943 in an article entitled 'Defining the field at a given time', published in the *Psychological Review*, Lewin described what is now known as force field analysis. This is a tool that you can use to anticipate resistance to change and plan to overcome it (see Figure 8.2).

Monitoring staff morale

One way to both identify resistance to cost-cutting changes and to keep track of progress whilst implementing them is to carry out regular surveys of employee attitudes, opinions and feelings. HR-Survey (www.hr-survey.com > Employee Opinions) and Custom Insight (www.custominsight.com > View Samples > Sample employee satisfaction survey) provide fast, simple and easy-to-use software to carry out and analyse human resources surveys. They

What is the problem/ change issue?			
Where are we now?			
Where do we want to get to?			
What/who are the main forces at work	Driving Forces	Neutral Forces	Resisting Forces
What action can we take to help driving forces, encourage neutral forces to help and to overcome resisting forces			

Figure 8.2 Force field analysis template

both have a range of examples of surveys that you can see and try before you buy, which may stimulate your thinking.

Recognize that major cost cuts take longer than expected to deliver their benefits

Researchers Adams, Hayes and Hopson explain in *Transition: Understanding and Managing Personal Change* (Martin Robinson, London, 1976) the stages that people go through when experiencing change and hence the reason the process takes so long. The stages are: immobilization or shock, disbelief, depression, acceptance of reality, testing out the new situation, rationalizing why it's happening, and then final acceptance. Most major changes make things worse before they make them better. More often than not, the immediate impact of change is a decrease in productivity as people struggle to cope with new ways of working and whilst they move up their own learning curve. The doubters will gloat and even the change champions may waver. But the greatest danger now is pulling the plug on the plan and either adopting a new plan or reverting to the status quo. To prevent this 'disappointment' it is vital both to set realistic goals for the change period and to anticipate the time lag between change and results.

Cost-cutting assignment 8

Go back over this chapter and look for ways to get cost cutting into the heart of your everyday business life.

1 How do you forecast revenues and costs; is it a satisfactory method accommodating trends, seasonality and allowing for random factors; and do you look far enough ahead?
2 Does your budgeting and reporting system work from a cost perspective in that you have variance reporting and flexed budgets?
3 Should you use zero-base budgeting in some or all areas of cost?
4 What steps do you take to benchmark your cost structures against the best-performing organizations in your sector?
5 Have you set priorities for your cost-cutting plans?
6 Who is likely to be most affected by your cost-cutting plans and what can be done to get them onside or at least limit their ability to disrupt your plans?

Index